# The Clinical Interview
## of the Child

# THE
# CLINICAL INTERVIEW
# OF THE CHILD

Stanley I. Greenspan, M.D.

*with the collaboration of*
*Nancy Thorndike Greenspan*

MCGRAW-HILL BOOK COMPANY

*New York · St. Louis · San Francisco*
*Auckland · Bogotá · Düsseldorf · Johannesburg · London*
*Madrid · Mexico · Montreal · New Delhi · Panama*
*Paris · São Paulo · Singapore · Sydney · Tokyo · Toronto*

This book was written by Stanley I. Greenspan, M.D. in his private capacity. No official support or endorsement by the National Institute of Mental Health, Department of Health and Human Services, is intended or should be inferred.

Lawrence B. Apple, Suzette H. Annin, Thomas H. Quinn, and Michael Hennelly were the editors of this book. Christopher Simon was the designer. Thomas G. Kowalczyk supervised the production. It was set in Times Roman with display lines in Perpetua by Com Com, Inc.

Printed and bound by R. R. Donnelley and Sons, Inc.


LIBRARY OF CONGRESS CATALOGING IN PUBLICATION DATA

Greenspan, Stanley I
    The clinical interview of the child.

    Bibliography: p.
    Includes index.
    1. Child psychopathology—Diagnosis.   2. Inter-
viewing in psychiatry.   3. Child psychology.   I. Greenspan, Nancy Thorndike, joint author.   II. Title.
[DNLM: 1. Interview, Psychological—In infancy and
childhood.   WS 105 G815c]
RJ503.5.G73      618.92'89075      80–39736
                        AACR1


2 3 4 5 6 7 8 9 DODO 8 0 7 6 5 4 3 2

ISBN 0-07-024340-9

*To our parents*
*who began our education*
*and our children, Elizabeth and Jake,*
*who enthusiastically continue it.*

# Contents

# The Clinical Interview
of the Child

# Chapter 1

# Conceptual Foundations: An Overview

The clinical interview with the child presents an unusual challenge and opportunity. The challenge lies in the fact that children are complicated and yet, once their modes of communication are understood, at the same time straightforward. To the extent that the clinician is able to meet the challenge successfully, the clinical interview allows unique access to the child's highly individual world and special experiences, opening the way to accurate diagnosis and effective therapy.

Surprisingly enough, one of the main talents the clinician must possess is knowing how to stay out of the child's way as he reveals, at his own pace and in his own "words," the character and contents of his experiential world. At the same time the talented clinician will know when and how to step in and help the child communicate in an increasingly rich and personal manner. Being naturally ingenious, children will share their thoughts and feelings with the clinician through a variety of communication channels. The clinician's task is to be tuned in to all of these channels simultaneously and to be alert to every nuance of meaning conveyed.

The clinician must therefore be a highly skilled observer, which includes seeing, hearing and in other ways sensing all of the data the child provides. A basic requisite of being a good observer is to resist the very human tendency to jump to conclusions on the basis of insufficient evidence and thus propose premature formulations. Do not rush to explain your observations. Ask yourself questions and use hypotheses to test your understanding. Only when all the pertinent information is in should you formulate a diagnosis. Otherwise you may overlook important aspects of the child's personality.

As indicated, the basic requirement of a good clinician is the ability to observe in several dimensions simultaneously. Children communicate through the way they look at—or avoid looking at—the clinician, the style and depth of their personal relatedness, their mood, the variety and types of emotions they manifest, the way they negotiate the space of the interview setting, the themes they develop in talk and play, and in many other ways as well. The organization, depth, age-appropriate relevance, and sequence of the child's affects and themes are all vehicles for sharing the structure, character, and contents of his or her experience. A good observer must therefore continuously monitor every communication channel—both verbal and nonverbal—that the child employs throughout their time together.

In the following chapters the principles and methods of systematic observation will be discussed in detail. Then consideration will be given to the way in which these observations lead to clinical judgments. Before turning to these practical matters, however, it will be useful to review a few general concepts of human behavior.

## Multiple Lines of Development

It is universally acknowledged among mental health professionals that personality develops along multiple lines. Development in the overall physical, neurological, cognitive, and intellectual realms, as well as the development of human relationships, coping strategies, and general styles of organizing and differentiating thoughts, wishes, and feelings—all these areas of development and more contribute to the ways one organizes and creates one's unique experience of life. Agreement on the most salient half-dozen areas could easily be reached; after that, various special frames of reference —e.g., social adaptation, family patterns—would augment the list differentially for various clinicians. The only disputes that arise in this general consensus about the multiplicity of developmental lines concern which of this or that proffered conceptualization helps us better understand human functioning. Some clinicians might emphasize the person's relationship to the external environment, the family, and other social structures; others might emphasize the person's intrapsychic, experiential world. Some might champion the primacy of the cognitive, intellectual processes whereas others would favor the emotional processes. None would disagree, however, that each of these areas participates in the whole and demands consideration, particularly when one is trying to assess the total personality.

Unfortunately, theoretical acceptance of multiple lines of development is not matched by practical adherence, as is notable in many of our attempts at conducting the clinical examination—especially for research but also for clinical purposes. Thus too often an emphasis on the behavioral level is permitted to overshadow the experiential level, or a focus on the superficial aspects of social adaptation is allowed to exclude adequate consideration of how a person deals with deeply experienced feelings. An example will illustrate this point. Some young people who are class leaders, assertive and viewed by their peers and teachers as very competent, and who in general manifest behaviors consistent with highly successful and skillful social adaptation, may nevertheless develop severe depressions and even psychotic disorganizations. Some of these adolescents who were studied in depth were found to have had lifelong problems in handling certain deeply felt feelings involving passive longing, dependency, and intimacy. Insofar as the concept of multiple lines of development is paid lip service but not adhered to in a rigorous manner, clinical evaluations will tend to miss these subtler dimensions of human functioning.

To avoid being overwhelmed by complexities, the clinical interviewer must have a conceptual framework that will alert him to the different dimensions of functioning that will emerge in the clinical setting. Anna Freud (1965) has written an extraordinarily useful book, *Normality and Pathology in Childhood,* in which she delineates a number of developmental lines that can be useful in conceptualizing various dimensions of the child's behavior and experience. Likewise, Erik Erikson's (1950) work on the delineation of psychosocial stages, Margaret Mahler's (1975) work on the development and individuation of the self and the role of early object relations, and Jean Piaget's work on cognitive developmental stages are noteworthy contributions that delineate the developmental progression characteristic of different areas of personality functioning.

The point I wish to underscore in introducing this volume is that a child's personality, no less than that of an adult, comprises many interrelated lines of development. It must also be remembered that, although these lines can be arbitrarily separated for conceptual purposes, in the functioning experience of a child they are all interrelated.

## Multiple Determinants of Behavior

Another principle worthy of attention in these introductory comments is that every discrete behavior is multiply determined. In other words, when viewing human functioning it is an oversimplification or error to assume a one-to-one relationship between what is observed and some real or hypothesized causal factor.

For example, a child may be angry one day because a friend took his favorite game. He may be angry on another day because a girl flirted with him and he became sexually aroused. He may become angry at another time because he cannot understand the teacher's math instructions. On still another day he may be angry because his visiting grandparents have now gone home. And on yet another day he may be angry for all those reasons at once. This child may demonstrate his anger by throwing chalk at the blackboard on each of these occasions, and his chalk throwing may be the only behavior observed. Yet this single act of anger may be related to one of several different causes or to a combination of any number of them at a given time.

Similarly, a child may represent the same feeling or the same internal state with different behaviors. The child who feels angry in response to his father's belittling and making fun of him may behave provocatively. At another time, his reaction to this same type of humiliation may take the form of compliance and passivity. At still another time, he may behave competitively or in a disorganized way. Thus, an internal feeling of humiliation and anger may manifest itself in four or five different ways depending on the contextual situations or on other related internal states the child is experiencing.

In sum, this principle of multiple determination suggests that there are multiple relationships between what clinicians observe and the way children organize their experiential world.

4

### The Developmental Structuralist Approach: A Brief Summary

As one considers the multiple determinants of behavior and the multiple lines of development, it becomes increasingly necessary to have a model or a way of viewing development that is both sensitive to the complexities inherent in these concepts and useful to clinicians in their tasks of direct observation of children's experience. The developmental structuralist approach focuses on how a person organizes experience at each stage of development. Experience is broadly defined to encompass emotional experience as well as experience with the inanimate or impersonal world. The person's experiential organization is the final common pathway for multiple determinants (environmental, biological, etc.) that influence behavior and can be studied in relation to each specific line of development. The developmental structuralist approach, which is elaborated in *Intelligence and Adaptation* and related works (Greenspan, 1979, in press), will be only briefly discussed here.

Before describing this approach, it should be highlighted that for the reader not interested in theory, it is quite appropriate to skip this section and resume on p. 15. Two assumptions are related to this approach. One is that a person's organizational capacity progresses to higher levels as he or she matures. "Higher levels" in this context implies an ability to organize in stable patterns an increasingly wide and complex range of experience. The interplay between age-appropriate experience and maturation of the central nervous system ultimately determines the characteristics of this organizational capacity at each phase. The second assumption is that, for each phase of development, in addition to a characteristic organizational level, there are also certain characteristic types of experience (e.g., interests or inclinations) that "play themselves out," so to speak, within the organizational structure. Stage-specific experiences or inclinations are evidenced in the stage-specific types of wishes, fears, curiosities, and inclinations—often referred to as drives, psychosocial tasks, etc.[1] Stage-specific experiences are also related to the interplay of biological maturational processes and ongoing experience with the environment.

We therefore focus on *two* components of a person's experiential world.

---

[1]The model being described here is a biological adaptational one, in that the adapting individual develops his or her unique experiential organizations and "contents" from an interplay in which maturational progression and its phase-specific inclinations operate on and are responded to by the environment.

One component is the level of organization of experience. For example, we would expect an 8-year-old to organize her experience sufficiently to be able to separate reality from fantasy, modulate impulses, regulate mood, focus concentration, integrate thoughts and emotions, delineate—in an ever-subtler fashion—her sense of self from her sense of others, and maintain her self-esteem. The above abilities are the age-appropriate organizational features that characterize the adaptive experiential organization of an 8-year-old. In contrast, a maladaptive organization would be characterized by the tendency toward disorganization with vulnerable reality testing or impulse regulation.

The second component of a person's experiential world relates to the *type* of experience organized. Here one looks at the specific thoughts, concerns, inclinations, wishes, fears, and so forth. The type of experience is, in a sense, the drama the child is experiencing, whereas the organizational level might be viewed metaphorically as the stage on which this drama is being played. To carry this metaphor a step further, it is possible to imagine some stages which are large and stable and therefore can support a complex and intense drama. In comparison, other stages may be narrow or small and thus able to contain only a very restricted drama. Still other stages may have cracks in them or crumble easily under the pressure of an intense, rich, and varied drama.

According to the developmental structuralist approach, at each phase of development there are certain characteristics that define the experiential organizational capacity, i.e., the stability and contour of the stage. At the same time there are certain age-appropriate dramas or themes characterized by their complexity, richness, depth, and content. This approach then provides a set of expectations and clinical-indicator behaviors or capacities for each age or developmental stage. It focuses on adaptive capacities expected as well as on limitations and conflicts.

*Specific Lines of Development*

Each organizational level and type of experience may be studied in relationship to a number of different lines of development. Abstract notions can thereby be brought down to a concrete level, particularly if the lines of development one chooses have directly observable clinical referents. For example, in looking at physical and neurological development, one may study the child's development of gross motor capacities, fine motor capacities, perceptual-motor coordinating capacities, higher-level central nervous system integrative capacities, and particular stylistic preferences at different ages. The landmarks for adaptive and maladaptive patterns are well known (and will be described in Chapter 3).

In looking at organizational levels one may also consider the development of human relationships. The infant progresses from a general interest in both the inanimate and the human world, to a specific and preferred interest in primary caretakers (often referred to as a primary attachment), to a capacity to differentiate the primary caretakers from others, to an ability to relate to the primary caretakers with a deepening sense of pleasure as well as protest and assertion. We observe for example the toddler develop—as part of his unfolding relationship capacities—the ability to integrate desires for closeness, intimacy, and dependency with the interest in curious, independent, assertive exploration of the world. It is also possible to delineate the age-appropriate organizational levels and unique experiential patterns for such as affects, anxiety, and thematic communication capacities.

It is important to keep in mind the distinction between the child's capacity for a certain organizational level along each developmental line and the child's particular experiential orientation—the content of his or her particular drama. For example, one possibility is for the child to achieve a level of development in human relationships where dependency and intimacy can be organized in a balanced and harmonious way with tendencies toward independence, mastery, and exploration: witness the 15-month-old toddler who can joyfully explore the rooms in the house alone and then comfortably return to mother or father or other primary caretakers for pleasurable, secure interchanges (or at times not so pleasurable, but nonetheless intimate interchanges).

In contrast, another child may be totally chaotic and fragmented, with no purposefulness, or can only experience clinging dependency, holding onto mother's or father's leg and refusing to explore the world; still another child may be impervious to mother, father, and other people and seems only to explore the inanimate world with a calm, almost bland, resolve that leads the observer to question the level of interest or pleasure this child is experiencing.

A determination should be made about the range of experience a child can organize before the drama that child may choose to play out is considered. The first child, who is capable of integrating within his experiential organization (in terms of the line of development concerned with human

7

relationships) intimacy as well as some relative independence, may choose or show a preference for a drama that has to do with zooming cars. Another child may show preference for a drama that has to do with dolls falling off chairs or with peekaboo games. While the particular drama—the contents of the child's communications or play—is very interesting and important, it should not be confused with an independent determination of the child's organizational level of experience. While there *are* characteristic dramas or themes that tend to reflect certain phases of development, it is important to point out that the content of the dramas varies widely because it is determined by both experiential (environmental) and biological factors. Nonetheless, if one constructs categories broadly enough, one does tend to see general trends characteristic of different levels of organization. The relative universality of the Oedipal drama would be an example of such a trend.

### Abstracted Formulations

As suggested above, the organizational level as well as the particular types of experience a child embraces can be delineated for each separate developmental line. At a descriptive level, looking at the child's physical and neurological capacities and inclinations, relationships, affects and emotions, thematic communication patterns, and so forth, affords a very well-discriminated, detailed view of the child.

At the same time the developmental structuralist model also lends itself to abstracting from these highly detailed observations of the child's organizational level and experiential orientation in each line, categories reflecting overall developmental status. These categories of functioning may be viewed on a spectrum from maladaptive to adaptive organizational patterns. At one extreme, for example, there are defects in organizational integrity. A determination of a personality defect would be made when there is a severe impairment in the age-appropriate level of "core" personality or ego functions, such as reality testing, mood regulation, impulse modulation. Such defects in the ability to organize experience according to age-appropriate levels often occur as a result of faulty development in the first 3 to 4 years of life when such basic organizational capacities are being developed. The specific types of defects that stem from faulty development at each period of early development will be discussed in detail later.

Another level of maladaptive development may be summarized under the category of constrictions in the flexibility of the personality. In this category there are no major defects in age-appropriate organizational capacities, but the range of experience that can be organized is restricted. For example, a 5-year-old child may have the capacity to test reality, but only in the context of very impersonal, shallow relationships and with affects of low intensity or affects restricted to the aggressive or negativistic domains. To use the metaphor of the stage and drama again, the stage does not have cracks in it and is not vulnerable to crumbling, but is extraordinarily narrow and therefore accommodates only a very restricted drama.

We may see restrictions ranging from severe ones based on compromises made early in life to minor ones stemming from later compromises. For example, there is a difference between persons who can maintain the integrity of their organizational capacities (the capacity for reality testing) only by totally walling off all human intimacy, and those who have minor limitations in experiencing assertive feelings with authority figures but otherwise function in an adaptive, age-appropriate way. The latter type of child simply may not be able to compete fully, whereas the former type of child realizes only a shadow of his or her human potential. The various types of constrictions will be described later (e.g., limiting the experience of certain types of feelings or thoughts, externalizing internal experiences).

A third, very subtle type of constrictive impairment is called an *encapsulated disorder,* based on the child's inability to maintain experiential continuity over time in narrowly delineated areas of experience, only minimally compromising the overall age-appropriate flexibility of personality.

Once a judgment is made about the child's level and type of organizational defect and/or constriction, one can then categorize the type of drama being played out. Dramas, some of which are quite painful, may play themselves out in age-appropriate, adaptive experiential organizations (e.g., phase-specific conflicts); less painful dramas may play themselves out in very constricted or even defective organizations.

In summary, experience may be organized at different levels; each level may have its own stylistic uniqueness; and each line of human development (delineated according to clinically meaningful categories) may be described in terms of its organizational level and its experiential uniqueness. Detailed observations of each line of development may be abstracted into a formulation about the overall level of personality functioning in terms of personality defects and constrictions, as well as adaptive, age-appropriate patterns.

*The Developmental Structuralist Approach in*
*Other Models of Development*

The developmental structuralist approach, which focuses attention on the organization and content of experience, is compatible with most models of human behavior. For example, in psychoanalytic or psychodynamic approaches, the focus on dynamic, structural, genetic, and ego-psychological perspectives is related to the maturational and experiential properties of the personality. For example, the dynamic perspective focuses on the relationship of a person's drives or wishes to the fears, internalized prohibitions, reality constraints, and defense mechanisms of the personality. The dynamic perspective therefore becomes a "window" through which to study certain unique experiences. The genetic perspective orients us toward the historical unfolding of dynamic trends and is consistent with the biological adaptational approach suggested earlier. The structural and ego-psychological perspectives, which also focus our attention on conflict, alert us to the mediating properties of the ego—its ability to synthesize the person's drives or wishes, fears, internalized prohibitions, and reality considerations. The ego's defensive operations and integrating and synthesizing capacities can be studied from this perspective.

Psychodynamic approaches also embrace object-relations theory. Object-relations theory formulates the way early relationship patterns are internalized into self- and object representations, and how these internalizations form the foundation for basic personality functions. Object-relations theory explains how certain organizational capacities of the personality are achieved.

This very brief overview is provided to suggest that the theoretical perspective of this work is compatible with and encompasses important psychodynamic viewpoints, and thus orients the skilled clinician to a microscopic examination of the organizational level and experiential uniqueness of the child.

At another extreme are behavioral and behavioral-learning approaches. These approaches, which focus on observable behavior rather than on internal experience, and on the environmental factors that appear to influence behavior through their contextual or temporal relationship to behavior, seem to be diametrically opposed to psychodynamic perspectives. Quite to the contrary, they provide a complementary orientation for whose theoretical rationale I have described elsewhere (Greenspan, 1975).

In considering behavioral approaches, which are highly focused on environmental influences, it should be emphasized that a developmental model is needed to understand both the behavioral repertoire of the growing child at each phase of development and the likelihood that certain events will be experienced as reinforcing. Children are not simply a product of what they experience at any moment in time—or of past experiences, for that matter—but rather, of their capacities to *organize* experience at certain levels. The model presented here, which attempts to delineate the particular way children organize experience at each level of development, in a sense provides a picture of age-appropriate behavioral repertoires and potential categories of reinforcing events—or to put it more broadly, experiential repertoires.

In behavioral learning terms, these experiential repertoires can be viewed from the perspective of their organizational level and "content" uniqueness. For example, in using a behavioral learning approach with a child one first needs to make a determination regarding which categories of behavior to change. One does not wish to help a passive child be more assertive when that child has a more fundamental difficulty in behaving realistically. In other words, if a child has a defect in the organizational capacity for reality testing—which at a behavioral level emerges through a tendency to behave unrealistically—that issue may require attention first. If the clinician misses the child's fundamental difficulty in "behaving realistically" because he lacks a conceptual framework for finding clinically relevant categories of behavior, the treatment approach that is formulated may exacerbate, rather than alleviate, the child's primary difficulty. The developmental structuralist approach therefore is not only compatible with behavioral approaches, but may aid in delineating the most clinically relevant "experiential" categories.

### Empirical Aspects of a Developmental Structuralist Approach

The developmental structuralist approach, though tied to a cohesive theory (see Greenspan, 1979), can also be used in an atheoretical, empirical manner. In a sense, the identification of the ways children organize experience and their phase-specific stylistic uniqueness at each level of development may be documented without regard to a particular theory. The usefulness of the observational categories described in Chapter 2 can be judged on their own merits in terms of their usefulness for clinical evaluation, planning, and following the course of treatment. The "acid test" would be their usefulness in a variety of research contexts: describing stage-specific behavior and making predictions about future behavior, predicting the treatment approaches likely to be effective with certain types of problems and individuals, etc. In other words, the validity of this approach can be empirically assessed by its application in a variety of clinical and research contexts.

### Relationship of the Developmental Structuralist Approach to Traditional Diagnostic Categories

As will be suggested later, the developmental structuralist approach can be used in conjunction with existing standard diagnostic categories. The existing diagnostic scheme of the American Psychiatric Association (1980), DSM-III, however, should be recognized as limited for assessing children because it lacks a cohesive developmental focus that encompasses multiple developmental lines. DSM-III takes into account only certain syndromes of childhood, and then only in an unsystematic way. It tends to base these syndromes either on symptoms clusters, personality traits, or an identification of etiological factors. For example, Axes I and II in the DSM-III approach, which focus on the syndromes and personality types, are not tied to a cohesive theory of human development that considers adaptation and maladaptation at each developmental level along a number of clinically relevant lines.

The developmental approach suggested here offers a potentially useful addition—a way to understand each child in terms of his or her developmental tendencies for each area of functioning. The categories that are suggested here may eventually substitute for Axes I and II in the current, formal DSM-III nomenclature. Optimally, a diagnostic approach to children should be a developmental one.

Currently, however, one may use the approach suggested here as a complement to the traditional diagnostic categories. As will be described later, one may consider a three-column approach, where symptom clustering and personality-trait-oriented diagnostic labels (Axes I and II from DSM-III) are represented in one column. In another column, diagnoses based on etiological factors may be represented (such diagnoses are rare, but are important to list when they are known—these are usually contained in Axis I of DSM-III). In yet a third column, one may list a developmental diagnosis based on how children organize and delineate their experiential world. We will see that developmental diagnoses are meaningful not only for diagnostic purposes but for clinical evaluation and planning, as well as for understanding etiological factors.

## General Principles

I began with the principles of multiple determinants of behavior and multiple lines of development—and suggested that we use the developmental structuralist model to explore these principles—in order to emphasize just how complex our task is in the clinical interview of a child. We are asked to determine not only what is troubling a child at a particular point in his or her development but also to understand the child's personality organization. The problem for an 8-year-old boy, for example, might be that he has conflicts with his mother, who is trying to keep him dependent while he wishes to move out and do more things on his own. Perhaps the boy is being negativistic and belligerent, and not working in school, and so comes in for an assessment.

Here, you not only have to assess the nature of the problem that precipitated the visit but you are also asked to assess any other issues that may be related. Even more important, you are also called on to assess the structure in which this current difficulty is occurring. How is this child functioning across the board, what kind of psychological or personality organization has this child achieved, and how does this organization compare with age-appropriate expectations? In other words, you are called on to make an assessment along multiple developmental lines; to describe the theater or stage, as it were, in which the current drama is being played out. To use a medical analogy, a physician needs to know the basic state of the patient's health before treating an infection. Treating an infection in a person with another chronic condition such as cancer is very different from treating an infection in a person who is otherwise healthy.

Mastering the complexity of the clinical diagnostic situation requires rigorous observation and conceptualization combined with patience. We must avoid the temptation to become too simplified in our approaches as a defense against our sense of just how complex life is in our area of work. One may throw up one's hands and say, if life is so complicated, if human beings are so complex in their functioning, and if the interview of the child demands that I be aware of multiple lines of development and multiple determinants of behavior, how am I ever to conclude anything? But rather than causing one to give up in despair, the complexity of human functioning should inspire the novice as well as the skilled clinician to rise to the occasion. The challenge will not be met with premature formulations or a narrowed focus that encompasses only a few dimensions of experience. Moreover, in the context of the clinical interview, the current vogue for too much operationalizing and quantifying of human behavior must be viewed as inconsistent with the processes necessary for a full understanding of the child's functioning.

The challenge presented by the clinical interview of the child can be met with an approach that is geared to unraveling complexity. In brief, interviewers must train themselves to monitor the multiple channels of communication used by the child; the data obtained will generate hypotheses that, through a process of gradual approximation, will clarify the problem in hand. The succeeding chapters outline the framework for simultaneously observing multiple dimensions of human functioning during the clinical interview, and describe, first, how to translate these observations into first-order clinical inferences and then how to derive clinical hypotheses and judgments from these inferences.

# Chapter 2

# Framework for Systematic Observation of the Child

In this chapter I detail a number of categories for observation during the interview. In each category, two levels of data are pertinent. One is the descriptive level; that is, accurate description of the observed behavior. The other is the age-appropriate level; that is, an assessor must have some sense of the age- or developmental stage-appropriate functioning for each of these categories so that departures from the range can be noticed.

The first category includes everything related to the physical integrity of the child. The next category involves the emotional tone of the child during the assessment. The third category concerns how the child relates to you as a human being during the interview. The fourth concerns the specific affects and anxieties that become elaborated during the initial clinical interview. The fifth category covers the way the child uses the environment of the waiting room and the playroom. The sixth deals with thematic development: the way the child develops themes in terms of depth, richness, organization, and—of great importance—sequence. The final category covers your subjective feelings—the reaction of the diagnostician to the child. The data in this last category concern the feelings the child evokes in you—both your general feelings at the end of the interview and any specific fantasies or feelings you experienced during the interview. These first-order observations should yield good data, and good data are basic to any hypotheses you may formulate.

Let me add that, although the examples that follow refer to an interview playroom setting, these observational categories can be used in any setting. A child on an inpatient unit or in a schoolroom, for example, can be observed from these multiple perspectives. You can notice how he relates to the other children, how he uses you, how he uses space, his physical and neurological status in terms of activity level and coordination, his mood and changing affects during the observation period. Although systematic observation is easier when you have a child alone—such as in a playroom session or in your own interview setting—it can be done in any setting. A teacher in a schoolroom can use this observational framework as effectively as a nurse on a hospital ward.

## Physical and Neurological Development

Let us now discuss each of the above-mentioned categories in detail, beginning with physical and neurological development. Here, you want to observe the level of the child's physical and neurological intactness in order to determine if further neurological or psychological assessment is needed. You can begin observation in the waiting room when you greet the child. You notice things like the child's posture, gait, balance, fine motor coordination, gross motor coordination, speech, and quality and tone of voice. You want to get any impressions you can about the child's sensory system. Is there any difficulty in hearing you or seeing you, any difficulty in experiencing sensations through touch? For instance, if a child is turning away and looks at you when you speak, he can hear.

You also want to look for sensorimotor coordination. Is this a clumsy child who has trouble integrating body movements? When you shake the child's hand, you can see how he meets your hand and whether he has decent hand-eye coordination. By watching the gait, you can see if certain large muscle groups and gross motor functioning are intact. Once in the playroom or interview setting, there will be an opportunity to see fine motor coordination when the child picks up some drawing material. If the child avoids that material, at some point in the interview you might suggest drawing in order to see his fine motor coordination.

You want to look at the child's overall physical well-being in terms of height, weight, skin tone, and general health. You should observe the activity level of the child, not only at the beginning of the interview but throughout it. Is this a child who shows some variation in activity level around certain tasks—does she get excited or involved and then slow down and concentrate? Is the child extremely active and uncontrollable from the beginning of the interview, or very slow and passive in all activity? All these things you can observe at the beginning of the hour to get an initial impression, and then continue observing throughout the hour, noting any changes. Such changes are important, particularly if you want to make an assessment of a functional cause of some physical difficulty. With a child who has a questionable learning difficulty, for example, you may find, that though initially fine motor coordination and sensorimotor integration look good, when you hit on some anxiety-arousing area, all of a sudden the child falls apart. Such data suggest that some issues in the emotional sphere interfere with certain physical capabilities.

One can perform a very general neurological examination without laying hands on the child. There is much to be observed about the functioning of the physical and neurological systems. For instance, if you observe some spasticity you can wonder about cerebral palsy of a minor nature without having to test the child's reflexes. If you notice any unusual weaknesses in a limb or on one side of the body, you should again be thinking in this way. Often, when we are doing a psychiatric evaluation, we assume the neurological functions are intact. We think it is none of our business, so we are not sensitive to noticing that a child favors the right side or has a weakness on the left side. This may not mean anything, but certainly one can use such an observation as the basis for questioning the family about this child's development in order to determine whether a neurological evaluation is necessary.

In another case, you may decide that psychological evaluation is necessary. For example, after you have entered the waiting room and introduced yourself to an 8-year-old girl, she jumps and skips back into the playroom, where she socks a bag a couple of times. When it comes to drawing, however, her fine motor coordination seems to be immature. Although she is 8 years old, she has trouble making letters. These observations may raise questions about whether there is some central nervous system immaturity or minimal dysfunction; you may want psychological testing to focus on this area.

In summary, even in your initial session you can reach the determination of whether a neurological workup is necessary, and what specific work you wish to have done in areas where you have questions. You should have a fairly good idea whether the psychological test results (e.g., the developmental level on the Bender Visual Motor Gestalt Test) are going to tell you something, and if you are surprised by them it should raise a diagnostic question. In other words, if you see a child whose physical and neurological integrity seem intact but whose developmental level on the Bender is very immature, you want to know why there is a discrepancy between your clinical observations and the test results.

### Mood

The next category deals with the mood or overall emotional tone. From the very beginning, you want to notice the child's mood, and then you want to watch how it evolves during the interview. It is different from the variations in affect or emotion that you will see throughout the interview. Your perception of the mood or general emotional tone will be an integrated judgment based on the way the child looks and behaves as well as on the content of his or her speech. Looking at mood from outside the clinical context for a moment, you may feel that a friend is depressed, based on observation of many aspects of that person's behavior. The person may talk about happy events but look sad, move sluggishly, and make occasional veiled comments about whether life is worth living. Taken all together, your observations indicate that the person is depressed.

In determining the child's mood, you should use any behavioral references you have to construct an overall picture. Facial expression is a good example. You can see if the child is sad-looking, sits in a corner and is not involved with anyone in the waiting room; or if the child is cheerful, a little hypermanic, and optimistic about the world. Often the mood you perceive is an intuitive impression because children rarely show certain moods (depression is an example) that are obvious in teenagers or adults.

The content of the interview is also relevant to the assessment of the mood. If you meet a sad, lonely-looking, 5-year-old girl who shakes hands limply, walks in passively and sits inertly, and then finally begins playing out themes involving destruction, you know that content supports the observations you have gathered about emotional tone or mood. If the child's themes evolve to feelings of helplessness—no matter how hard she tries, nothing goes right for her—the evidence is consistent with the overall mood.

Your own subjective feeling at the end of an interview can be extremely helpful in assessing a child's mood. Some leave you feeling depressed, and it is important not to rationalize and disregard your feeling by thinking, e.g., well, I'm tired, it's been a long day, or, I had a fight with my spouse earlier in the day. Other children leave you feeling invigorated, which is also a diagnostic clue. The seductive child who invigorates you; the sad, hungry child who leaves you feeling drained; and other children who evoke various other feelings—each child provides clues about mood by means of your subjective response. Any discrepancy between your observations and your subjective response may indicate that the overall emotional tone of the child is more complicated than it appears. You may want to have a second or a third diagnostic session, depending on how many questions remain unanswered after your first session.

### Human Relationship Capacity

The next category, relatedness to other persons, involves an examination of how the child relates to you. While you are with the child, you should observe how he or she treats you as a person, how your relationship develops, and how differentiated it is. As is true for all these categories, observations belonging to this category begin in the waiting room. As you enter the waiting room and relax for a minute between patients, you want to observe both the interaction between the child and whoever brought him and between the child and others in the room. Is he being affectionate, or withdrawn and aloof? Is he making contact with others; how much distance does he maintain from them? Simply by watching for half a minute or so, you get an impression of how the child has negotiated all the available human relationships in the waiting room.

Do not dismiss from consideration or excuse on situational grounds what the child has chosen to do. If you see a child who is clinging for dear life to mother's hand, ignoring the other adults and the playthings in the waiting area, you might wonder to yourself if this child is scared to death of coming to the hospital or office and seeing a psychiatrist. This snap impression should always take the form of a hypothesis. It is a mistake to formulate explanations so early in the clinical meeting. Do not fall into the trap of trying to explain the behavior before you have all the data.

While you are in the waiting room, it is also important to note your initial reaction to the family. With one family, we feel comfortable nodding to the mother and standing and observing for a few minutes, just relaxing between patients; we see no display of discomfort in the family. With another family, however, we find that as soon as they see us, we feel compelled to go to them immediately; we cannot have a cigarette to relax for a minute or take a few deep breaths between patients. We experience such a family as demanding our immediate attention and we are anxious to comply, as if we sense that they will be insulted and angry if we do not. Use this intuition as another clue to what is going on—even if you react to it, which is sometimes appropriate so as not to put too much stress on a family during a diagnostic phase.

After observing how the child relates to the people in the waiting room and what your reaction to the family is, you should note how the child relates to you, human being to human being. How does the child greet you? Is she wide-eyed, asking how you are, eager to come along with you? Or, as soon as you enter, does the child run to the other side of the room, greet you with some caution and apprehension, yet show a willingness to come along, enough trust to come into the playroom without mother? Or does the child start crying and fussing, hold on to mother's leg, and demand that she come into the playroom with her? What is the first feeling tone between the two of you as people? Is it a twinkle of acceptance in the child's eye, but with some anxious glances toward mother, thus showing you a combination of interest and apprehension?

It is the extremes that should be noticed here. You cannot expect to appreciate subtleties in a few minutes, but you can certainly pick up on the aloof, distant child who does not want to make contact with you at all. Such observations will give you clues about the areas you may want to explore. For example, I remember seeing one 3-year-old girl who took my hand as if I were a long-lost favorite uncle she had been waiting to see. I felt good because so many children greet one quite differently. But the way this child took my hand and came skipping along to the playroom made me feel almost too tremendously accepted. She did not show the normal wariness of a stranger. Subsequently this behavior proved to be a clue to the fact that the child was emotionally promiscuous in relating to people. You will see this kind of global emotional hunger and lack of discrimination in relating to people in some children with a history of early deprivation.

As you gain experience, you will get a sense of the initial types of behavior acceptable from a new patient, child or adult. Often the first tip-off to a borderline or psychotic problem occurs in the first few minutes of the interview when the child does something that you cannot quite identify because it is outside the realm of normal, acceptable opening moves. (Of course, "acceptable" opening moves are not delineated as such, but your intuition tells you something is amiss.) Again, having an unusual feeling is a clue to a diagnostic *question,* rather than leading to any conclusion.

Once the interview begins, does the child make contact with you at a personal level? Do you feel a personal sense of relatedness? Does that sense evolve, and at what point? Does the relatedness vary throughout the interview? Take a normal, healthy 6½-year-old child who may have some circumscribed neurotic problem. We might expect the child to start out cautiously, maybe warily, because you are a new person in his or her life. You may expect the child to warm up to you slowly during the interview; you will feel a sense of relatedness evolving. You will get a sense of this child as another human being. You will not feel that there is a mechanical quality or a distant, "not all there" quality. You will not feel an impersonal kind of hunger wherein the child regards and uses you as if you were just another object in the room like the guns or the toy animals. Instead, you feel a relationship beginning as you find yourself getting more interested in this child. By the end of the hour, different emotions and themes emerge and the relationship grows. You will feel that the two of you have made some emotional contact.

This prototypical child might be compared with one who is persistently aloof and emotionally detached, never making contact with you. Such a child may keep his back to you and maintain a distance of six or seven feet from you. He may be interested in some of the inanimate objects and games, he may even talk or look at you, but you never feel any sense of relatedness. A third type is the child who wants you to be there all the time, who is hungry for any human attention and involves you in everything.

In addition, you may observe subtler ways in which the child relates to you as a person, ways that are suggestive of certain characterological traits. For instance, you may see the child who wants to control you. As the interview begins, you get a sense of human relatedness, but then the child tries to control you. He or she gives you orders, has you play this game or that. You make a suggestion because you want to see the youngster draw. The child replies, "No, we are going to do this now," showing an orderly kind of obsessive behavior. Other boys and girls may be seductive and flirtatious in the way they engage you. You find yourself not only getting interested but even a little excited. You find you are enjoying yourself thoroughly, and if you allow them to continue, you may have some interesting fantasies. This kind of seductiveness is usually thought to happen across sexes in Oedipal-aged children: the boy will be seductive with the female interviewer, the girl with the male interviewer. But the same thing can also happen when therapist and child are of the same sex. Whatever the case, such observations will give you a clue to the child's style of relating.

Experience with many children will give you the basis to look with sensitivity at the nature of the relationship. A set of internal, intuitive norms will evolve for you.

Let us take the example of a child who starts by showing slight apprehension. First he glances tentatively at mother. Then he comes into the room, sits in the corner for a minute or two, and asks whether he can play with something. You nod approval, and he begins exploring the room. Through play his fantasy about children having operations in hospitals emerges. You make a comment, "I understand that kids can be scared that when they come to a hospital, they are going to get operated on." The boy looks frightened for a second and begins taking the dolls and playing out a drama with one doll operating on another doll.

Shortly thereafter, you suddenly sense the child moving closer to you, shortening by half the 8-foot distance he had been keeping. He begins inviting you to get involved in play with him, whereas before he played alone. He wants you to manipulate one of the dolls for him. You begin feeling more comfortable and the sense of apprehension diminishes. In this example, then, you have seen some growth and development in relatedness during the interview: from tentativeness, fear and wariness, to an elaboration of concerns that most people have with any new person, and then to some beginning sense of warmth. This particular scenario may be suggestive of a fairly well-integrated child.

An example of an opposite sequence may go something like this: The child starts off being intimate and close, comes in and hits the Bobo doll, then starts drawing some pictures and playing with the dolls. She begins to develop all kinds of interesting dynamic themes such as stuffing the mother and father dolls down the toilet bowl; you are taking a flurry of notes. But as the interview goes on, the child moves away and becomes aloof, perhaps more passive. You feel at the end that you have lost a quickly made friend. While you should not interfere with the sequence of events in the opening interview, do note and learn from them.

In short, there are many possible patterns of relatedness. To determine relatedness, note your own subjective feelings; how the child relates to people in the waiting room; how he or she uses you during the interview; the spatial distance the child keeps as well as the verbal and eye contact he or she makes; and the child's emotional reaction to you versus his or her reaction to play materials. Although you cannot generalize from such observations how the child forms all other relationships, you can note the obvious extremes—a detached, aloof, uninvolved child or a tense, hungry child who relates promiscuously—and the subtle gradations in between.

Age expectations must also be taken into account. While all children optimally would be expected to develop an engaging sense of human involvement over time, with younger children the relatedness may take on a more egocentric quality. By ages 4, 5, or 6, you may expect a capacity for more mutuality and even empathy.

## Affects and Anxiety

I have labeled the next category affects and anxiety. Here you want to observe both the specific emotions that get elaborated at the opening of the clinical interview and those that follow sequentially around particular activities. Again, you should begin observing the child in the waiting room and continue until you say good-bye and the child reengages with mother. Make at least a mental note of the different emotions the child shows. How does the child begin the session with you? What happens as he or she moves through the first third to the middle of the session, and then from the last third to saying good-bye? Follow the change in affect. For example: the child may come in showing apprehension and tentativeness; get warm and loving, and then competitive; show concern with issues of sibling jealousy and rivalry; and then express concern about separating from you toward the end of the interview. Here several specific feelings have been elaborated; in contrast, another youngster may show only one or two affects during the entire interview.

You want to be able to label all the different emotions you see in specified situations, and thus you may wish to take notes under headings for each of the categories. Some people feel that taking notes interferes with their involvement with the child and they prefer to rely on memory. In such instances, taking notes after the interview under systematic headings may prove useful. You may observe anger, competitiveness, envy, rage, compassion, empathy, affection, caring, emotional hunger, emotions expressing aggressive feelings, and emotions expressing passive yearnings.

The range and degrees of specific affects are very broad. In the aggressive domain, for example, one finds gradations from assertive behavior, to competitive behavior, to mildly aggressive behavior, to explosive and uncontrolled aggressive behavior. The same is true in the affectionate and caring domain, which ranges from promiscuous emotional hunger, to mild affection, to a sincere sense of warmth, to compassion, to the developmentally advanced emotion of empathy.

Children vary in the range of affect displayed. Some will show a wide range in the themes they develop. They may talk openly about warmth and pleasurable relationships, and indirectly about competition and envy. You will be able to see the dominant affects. Other children may be relatively quiet the whole time, displaying little emotion. There may be one isolated scene, such as the child's punching the Bobo doll and beanbag, which expresses the theme of loss.

In all cases you want to see how your observations fit in with what is to be expected of a child at his or her developmental stage. In a 3-year-old, for example, one does not expect as great a variety of differentiated affects as an 8-year-old would show. With a 3-year-old you can expect to see possessiveness, with some show of stubbornness and negativism. You can expect to see some capacity to share with you, but not more mature affects like empathy. By age 6 or 7, if you see negativism and aggression but no desire to explore, and no curiosity, assertiveness, or signs of empathy, you have to ask why the latter affects are missing.

You should observe and describe not only the range of affects but the richness and depth of affects. Are they superficial, as if the child is simply playacting or imitating someone? Or do they convey a sense of personal depth (i.e., you are able to empathize with the way the child is feeling)? Again, age expectations are important here. In a 3-year-old you expect some superficial imitation; by age 6 or 7 you expect to get a greater sense of the child's own personal affects.

You also want to get some picture of the age- and stage-appropriate stability of the affects. Is the child able to maintain an emotion throughout a reasonably lengthy period of communication with you? Or is the child emotionally labile, showing a wide range of affects (e.g., sadness, crying, elation, aggression) in a two-minute period?

You want to notice the context in which the affects arise. A child who is engaging you in a certain style of relatedness may also be developing certain themes. Do the affects make sense in a thematic way, or are they inappropriate? Is the child showing joy and pleasure while cutting up the mother doll? Or does the child show compassion while burying a doll in the sand because it has just "died"? You want to note if the affects vary in relationship to the themes.

What we can call anxiety is related to the affects. Anxiety is not directly observed in the child, but it can be inferred from signs of distress or disruption. The best clue to points of anxiety is an abrupt disruption in a developing theme, an ongoing style of relating, or a mannerism or gesture. During most play sessions, if you stay out of the child's way by not over-structuring the situation, you will see some disruption in activity when the child comes to an area that troubles her, and you will see what the disruptive pathway is like for her in terms of personality structure. Did she show disorganized thinking and looseness in communication (equivalent to looseness of association in adults); did she lose impulse control, throwing or spilling things, or become clinging and want you to hold her?

For example, a child is playing with the mother and father dolls and develops the theme of the dolls fighting. She then darts to the other side of the room and begins behaving in a disorganized way, throwing things or messing up the floor with paint. You say to the girl, "That is not permitted because one rule of the playroom is that you cannot destroy things." She continues doing it, obviously disorganized and out of control. Finally she is about to spill the paint on your new suit and you have to restrain her. Here you have seen a profound disorganization occur.

Some children handle their distress by switching activities but carrying on the same theme in a less frightening mode. Again, let us say a child first develops the fighting theme with the mother and father dolls. Then, through a series of intermediaries, he shifts to drawing. He draws a cartoon with mother and father fighting and then draws some pictures of a less aggressive nature, showing that he wants to move into something less frightening. Here you see the ability to continue to work in a less frightening mode; the child has not given up entirely or become disorganized.

At first you will not know the nature of the anxiety, which may be fear of bodily damage, or of separation, or of some even earlier global anxiety. But you will know when there has been a disruption. At this point you just want to note its occurrence. When you go back over your notes and see the sequence of themes and affects, you will get some hints as to what caused the disruption.

You can learn a great deal simply by noting the sequence in a playroom session. The sequence of themes following a disruption may tell you what the child's fear centers on (e.g., bodily damage, world destruction, losing one's sense of self, losing the love of another person, abandonment). A sequence might run as follows: the child plays with the doll, darts over to the other side of the room and gets a gun, frantically shoots it at the dart board, and then goes back to the doll and starts shooting its arm off. Thus the child works a new theme—using the gun for violence—into the old drama. You have a picture of apprehension and anxiety; the theme seems temporarily broken, but then the child returns to it. He has armed himself but is still coming back into the "family" (the dolls). The sequence may suggest that he was concerned with some danger for which he felt a gun would be helpful. Therefore, one may hypothesize that the child is more concerned with physical, bodily harm than with separation or a more global loss.

When the child becomes anxious, it is often the interviewer's tendency to comfort him or her right away. The comforting is usually more subtle than putting one's arm around the child and saying, "Now, now, things will get better." For example, after seeing some acute anxiety, the interviewer may quickly begin structuring the activity by saying, "Why don't we try this," or, "Let's play checkers." A more sophisticated tack is to ask the child a question which diverts attention from the source of the anxiety to another area. We may say, "You know, you haven't told me about school yet. Tell me, how do you get along with the other kids at school?"

To be sure, if a child is becoming disorganized and cannot reorganize without help, you may need to move in a supportive way to help her reorganize her thinking and impulses. You can say something empathic, indicating that you understand her experience. Your remark should not focus on what stirred her up, e.g., "I can see that you don't like Mom and Dad fighting." The child who has played out such a fight scene and is already disorganized may not be able to deal with such a comment at that time. But if you say, "I know kids sometimes want to throw things and spill things," you are focusing on the child's tendency to get out of control rather than on what is scaring her. At the same time you are moving in, you are engaging and talking to the child, who will feel somewhat reassured. Such a course is much more reassuring than changing the topic. Also, after such a comment the child may be able to tell you about other instances when she was out of control.

The important point to note in the above example is that, for diagnostic purposes, it is necessary to observe the child's difficulty in coping before you take any action. You can be certain that whatever the child's behavior is in the playroom, it is worse at home. The child is not going to be destroyed if you remain silent for another 20 seconds. And the ability of a child to pull herself out without your help is such a vital diagnostic pointer that it is worth allowing the child to experience a little discomfort. Your whole treatment recommendation may hinge on such an observation, especially in cases where you are not sure whether the child's problems are predominantly characterological or fall predominantly into the category of "borderline" psychopathology.

In summary, in addition to noting the child's specific range, richness, and depth of affects, it is equally important to observe their appropriateness in terms of the child's age and the themes being revealed. When play is disrupted by the emergence of troubling issues, you want to watch the child's reaction to the anxiety and the degree to which he can become reorganized without your help. Noting the themes that precede the disruption, as well as the sequence of those that follow it, should give you an indication of what the fears relate to.

### Use of the Environment

The next category covers the way a child uses the environment—first the waiting room and then the playroom. Space in the office includes you as a human being, the inanimate objects such as the games and toys, and the space itself. What the child has is a multifaceted vehicle for communicating with you. Implicitly you have said, "Look, you have this room, these toys, and me. Now using these things, tell me something in the next fifty or sixty minutes." All children, even ones as young as 3 or 4 years, understand that the interview is a time for them to tell you something.

One of the first things you want to observe is whether the child can integrate the entire room. Such an ability will give you a picture of the degree to which the child can synthesize and integrate different elements in his or her own personality. The ideal way to use the space would be for the child to take it all in at the beginning, then move around and develop a few different areas, and finally synthesize the different areas. That is, a child may start with a view of the whole setup and develop a little story here, a little story there, and at the end you may see her beginning to weave together the little worlds she has developed for you.

For example, a child comes into the playroom apprehensively, goes into one corner and reveals some anxiety about the situation, and then begins exploring the playroom. She goes around and checks everything, then picks a few favorite areas, optimally interweaving them and relating them to one another. She takes a policeman doll from one part of the room, mother and father dolls from another part, and a lion from still another, and relates them to a theme of a policeman protecting the mother and father from the lion. This child not only develops a relatedness to her environment but tries to integrate its various elements.

In contrast, an obsessive or fearful child might move into one corner and stay there for the entire session. Another child may go all over the place impulsively, touching base with everything but never developing any of the areas. How the child initially approaches the space and how he eventually deals with it are useful data for you to record.

What I have been suggesting so far is that there is a great deal to observe in the interview that is quite independent of content: the child's physical neurological status, way of relating to you, overall mood, specific affects (including the moments of disruption), and use of space. Without knowing anything about content, if you provide vivid descriptions in all these categories, you will know a considerable amount about the developmental stage of the child and about what areas may be causing him difficulty.

As you consider the next categories—the depth, relevance, and sequence of the child's thematic organization and your own subjective reactions—you will develop further data about the child. It is important to highlight, however, that many interviews with children focus only on the thematic sequence and do not take advantage of the full range of observational data available.

### Thematic Development

The kinds of data included in the next category, thematic development, are in some respects subtler than those discussed so far. They involve analysis of the child's themes in terms of organization, richness and depth, age-appropriate relevance, and sequence. Here the word *themes* refers not only to the content of verbal communication but also to all the ways the child communicates—through drawing, playing, and other activities. Attention to thematic development will tell you a great deal about the child's characterological structure as well as the specific conflicts that the child may be experiencing at the time you are assessing him or her.

It will also yield clues to the appropriate course of treatment for the child. A child may come in with many conflicts and yet reveal a certain self-access that may permit easy, rapid movement in a treatment process. Other children may come with few manifest difficulties but show severe constrictions in the way they approach their own psychological lives. Observations along these lines will influence your choice of therapeutic strategies as well as your expectations of what will happen in the initial phases of therapy.

In considering thematic development, look first at the overall organization in terms of the presence or absence of logical links connecting the thematic elements. This process would be equivalent to observing the organization of thinking in an adult, but with important differences. In order to use such an approach with children, you must have an understanding of normal development and know what to expect at each age. Whereas with an adult you deal with one standard—a certain minimum capacity to organize thinking—with a child the standards vary according to age, and you must weigh the organization of themes against the age-appropriate standard.

For instance, if an adult reveals tangentiality in thinking and mild loosening of associations, you begin getting a picture of some fragility of the personality structure. With a child, however, the meaning of such signs depends on age. In a 4-year-old, we might not be surprised by the absence of logical links; in a 3½-year-old we would be even less surprised. In children of 6, 7, and 8, however, we expect a greater capacity to form logical bridges between thematic productions.

Moreover, even after long experience in working with children, making age-appropriate judgments is not always straightforward. For example, it is very hard to know what degree of thematic organization is to be expected in an Oedipal child who is just at the point of moving on from the fantasy-oriented thinking that characterizes the early years and becoming capable of reality-oriented thinking. This developmental point lies in that gray area between what Piaget calls preoperational thinking and concrete operational thinking. Often you see latency children who are still under the pressure of fantasy. You are not sure if they believe what they are saying or if there are logical links organizing what they are communicating. The following cases are examples of age-appropriate and age-inappropriate thematic organization.

Let us say that you have an 8-year-old boy who comes into the playroom and begins, appropriately enough, by punching a beanbag; he then takes a gun, starts shooting a target, and talks about angry feelings; then suddenly he falls to the floor, takes off his pants, and shows you his genitals. The absence of thematic linking here would raise a question in your mind about the organization of this child's thinking. It is the abrupt departure from one theme to another rather than the content itself that would startle you. Although such abruptness in a 3½-year-old might be quite consistent with expectations, an 8-year-old who wants to talk about his body after talking about aggression ordinarily would move through a series of steps. For example, he would talk about shooting in general, about shooting the dolls, and about how the dolls are hurt; then he would draw a picture of a body, and with empathic questioning by the therapist, he might talk about fears regarding his own body.

Consider another example. A 9-year-old boy comes into the interview room, makes good eye contact with the examiner, smiles, and asks if there are any games or toys to play with. The examiner asks what he has in mind, and the boy says, "Do you have a basketball? I like to play basketball." The examiner responds empathically—"Oh" is enough—and the child is off and running, telling you that he played basketball today and made three baskets, etc.

As he talks about playing basketball, his emotional expression suddenly begins to get sad. When the interviewer wonders aloud about this change from glee and elation to a beginning look of sadness, the child says, "Well, I don't have enough friends to play with." He continues, "What a nice office you have here," and wonders if the therapist has children with whom he plays basketball. Then the child reflects on how often he has to play basketball by himself. Although he has a court near his house, his father will not play with him, nor will his brother, nor has he any friends that he can call on. Upon inquiry about his lack of friends, the boy describes a pattern of superficial relationships with schoolmates. Here we see an organized communication in the context of playing basketball, the theme being one of desire for greater emotional closeness and difficulty in achieving it comfortably. The theme is organized in that the elements emerge logically.

Let us continue this scenario—one in which we would have some question about the integrity of this child's organization of thinking. The child who has talked about playing basketball, and in this context about his loneliness, emotional hunger, desire for closeness, and lack of real friends, then wants to know if the interviewer will play basketball with him. When the interviewer asks how the child envisions this happening, he gleefully talks about their going out to the school yard and playing one-on-one.

Immediately following this remark, he says to the interviewer, "Can people die of heart attacks?" The interviewer wonders why that thought occurred to him and the child then says, "There was a car accident and people lost their arms and legs. Can robbers get into a building and steal?" When the interviewer asks for further elaboration, wondering what he means, the child stays on the topic of robbers getting into a building and stealing things. As the child talks about this, the interviewer finally gets the impression that the boy is talking about his concern over having something stolen from him.

In the foregoing example, we see an abrupt shift from the interwoven themes of basketball, the wish for closeness, and feelings of loneliness and isolation, to themes of heart attack, physical injury, and things being stolen. A breakdown in thematic organization is signified by the absence of the connecting links that one would expect from a 9-year-old. Whereas the first segment reflects a relatively good capacity for thematic organization, in the second segment the child shows a breakdown in this capacity. If the child had not experienced this breakdown, you could have expected transitions concerning other sports, people getting hurt in sports, and the general issue of physical injury, eventually getting to the issue of being robbed. Such an alternative sequence represents an appropriate series for a 9-year-old. Through an explicit logic he would reach the same endpoint. The fantasy material concerning heart attacks, car accidents, and severed limbs would become elaborated less "from left field" and more with a series of thematic links or bridges.

The richness and depth of thematic development also deserve attention. Thematic organization reveals the degree to which a child has an age-appropriate capacity for reality testing and organized thinking or communicating. The richness and depth of thematic productions, on the other hand, should reveal the characterological or neurotic constrictions in the range of thought and affect available to the child. The child who is capable of developing rich, deep, age-appropriate themes is telling you that he has access to a rich, deep intrapersonal life. The child whose story is frag-mented, superficial, or stereotyped, however, is telling you that conscious-ness of his or her intrapersonal life must be kept limited.

Soap operas and melodramas, with their shallow plots and cardboard characters, fail to convey a sense of richness and depth. By contrast, a novel is considered great to the extent that it attains that sense. In a similar fashion, a child's thematic development, as it unfolds in the clinical inter-view, may range from being superficial and fragmented to being complex and meaningful.

Let us say we have a 7-year-old girl whose early development was trou-bled and whose Oedipal phase was poorly negotiated. Only partial closure was achieved at the expense of a great deal of inhibition around various sectors of the personality, such as anger, assertion, and even empathy or concern. In watching this child, you may see a lot of scattered associations. She may go for the doll and then go play with the gun, then start to draw a house. What will be notable is that you will not see any development of themes. In other words, there will be no unfolding of a story. Now even though a child, unlike an adult, does not tell you an organized story with feeling, if you sit with a child and do not interfere with what she does, a story of one kind or another will surely unfold.

A child such as this 7-year-old, who can portray only shallow bits and pieces of a drama, may be demonstrating many developmental blockages. The girl wants to tell more about her angry feelings, yet that leads to anxiety; she wants to tell more about some caring feelings, but that leads to anxiety; she wants to tell more about fears that she experiences (all indirectly, to be sure) and that way is blocked. Thus you may see a scatter of thematic material at a superficial level.

Admittedly, this lack of depth is hard to diagnose. It cannot be diagnosed simply by noting that the child moves to many different parts of the room or uses many different materials. Even though a child may behave in an active and even anxious way during the session, you can often see progres-sion in the development of a theme. You have to ask, what kind of under-standing did I get? how deep and rich was the material that this child was able to portray for me? These reflections will give you a picture of the degree of potential restrictions.

Here, too, in assessing the richness and depth of thematic development, you need to know the age-appropriate expectations. For example, from a latency child of 7½ or 8 you should expect some constricted thematic development, at least in the first diagnostic playroom interview, because of the nature of the defenses developed during latency. In such children you often see support of the repression that follows the Oedipal phase, with the use of reaction formations, and sometimes even the beginning of some isolation of affects. You may expect that latency children will fend you off, protecting their turf. However, the way in which they protect their turf may have a certain richness and depth to it. While taking the stand, "I'm not going to tell you everything you want to know and don't ask me too many personal questions at this time," they may yet be giving you a sense of their flexibility.

An Oedipal child, on the other hand, is usually capable of rich elaboration of fantasy. Some people think the Oedipal stage is the most creative time in one's life because of the abundant availability of thematic material. If you see a 5-year-old who is shallow and constricted you would certainly have questions. As you work with 5-year-olds, you will readily see the ease with which they get into a great variety of material; a lack of such easy variety may be a signal that there are developmental interferences or conflicts.

For example: a 5-year-old boy may come in, look at you, make meaningful eye contact, sit down, and ask, "What am I supposed to do?" When you ask him what his guess is, he may say, "Oh, I'm supposed to talk about my worries and fears." He spots a gun over in the corner of the room and asks, "Can I play with that?" After the interviewer nods affirmatively, the boy goes over and picks up the gun. He then begins a game of shooting the mother doll and the father doll, as well as going "bang, bang" at the interviewer.

Following the game of shooting, he takes the baby doll and puts it in a safe place in the corner of the room without comment. The interviewer wonders out loud, "Gee, you are putting the baby doll over in that corner of the room." The child replies, "Yes, I want to make sure it is safe." The interviewer says, "You mean from all the shooting?" The boy replies, "I don't want it to be hurt." The interviewer says, "How's that?" and the little boy goes over and gets the doctor kit out and begins taking care of the baby doll, bandaging it and making sure it is all right. He explains that the doll got caught in the cross fire, had its legs and arms cut off, and had an injury to its nose. In talking about the doll being hurt, he conveys some pretended sadness and then decides, "I'm going to get the robbers who did that."

He then sets up a game where he is a policeman shooting it out with the

33

bad guys. Following this, he talks about how people have to be careful about bad guys who "steal things." The therapist empathically says, "Yes, I can understand how one could be concerned about controlling those bad guys who steal things." At this, the boy elaborates on all the things that bad guys would want to steal—his television set, his money, and more, finally getting to his baby brother. As the interview progresses, he continues to develop the themes of bad guys stealing, and policeman and good guys protecting.

Then the child becomes curious about what is going on behind the doors of the interview room. The interviewer asks what he thinks is going on. He says, "I don't know," and then goes over to the dolls and develops a complicated interaction where the mother and father doll are fistfighting and then go into the bathroom together. This sequence continues as he develops more themes related to what mother and father do together and what they do in the bathroom.

The foregoing example shows a child capable of developing an organized, rich, deep drama. His story contains violence and protection (e.g., robbers and cops), and it reveals the various sides of his own wishes: to take things, to rob, and to protect the family against such wishes and impulses. He then reflects on a theme related to his interests in robbing and protecting, that is, what goes on behind closed doors. His story shows his curiosity about his parents, what they do in the bathroom and other rooms that are closed off to him. Here is an example of the development of themes (which are also appropriate for a child of this age) that gets richer and deeper as the interview goes along.

Consider a contrasting illustration. A 5-year-old boy comes in and starts the interview in the same way as the first child: he goes after the gun and shoots it, and then sees the Bobo doll in the corner and starts punching it. The boy shoots and punches the Bobo for the next 15 minutes. The interviewer comments, "Gee, you really enjoy shooting and punching the Bobo." The boy looks at the interviewer as though to nod in agreement and continues the shooting and punching. Finally tired of the Bobo, the child goes around and shoots up the various dolls and the room in general. The interviewer again comments on the boy's desire to shoot, the child again gives a look to the interviewer indicating agreement and continues shooting.

The child sees a ball and asks the interviewer to play catch with him. They begin to throw the ball back and forth. The interviewer tries a number of times to have the child verbalize or develop in a richer way what might be on his mind, but the child sticks to alternating between throwing a ball and shooting the gun at the Bobo and other targets. Throughout this period, the boy makes good eye contact and seems reasonably affable. He is willing to come physically close to the interviewer. Near the end of the interview, desperate to get some more material, the interviewer suggests drawing, and the child draws a picture of a gun shooting a house. He then draws a picture of a child throwing a ball.

Here we have an example of a child who clearly shows that the theme of aggression (hitting and shooting) is on his mind, but we could say that there is very little richness or depth to the theme. What develops in the first few minutes of the interview is not further developed; rather, there is a repetitive quality to the child's communications, or thematic development, in contrast to the earlier example of ever-increasing richness and depth.

As mentioned earlier, you would not necessarily expect the same type of thematic depth and richness in an 8½-year-old as you would in a 5-year-old. An 8- or 9-year-old's personality ordinarily tends to be a little more rigid and stereotyped. Indeed, the competent latency-age child may successfully defend against many interesting fantasies. For example, an 8-year-old girl may come into the interview room and say, "I don't know why I am here. I haven't much to talk about." Then she may show some interest in playing checkers with the interviewer. There may be some discussion of the rules of the game which the child brings up—she wants to be sure that "we both understand in advance." As the rules of the game are elaborated, we see the child go into great detail, making sure that neither she nor the interviewer cheats. The interviewer inquires further about the importance of rules in connection with cheating. The girl then describes in elaborate detail the various ways one can cheat in playing different games. She talks about how friends at school sometimes cheat and says, "I have to be the one who is careful and not let them get away with it." The theme of cheating is also elaborated in terms of her 5-year-old brother who, she says, "likes to take advantage of me sometimes. He steals my things and gets into my games. I have to be careful of him." This theme then gets developed in terms of other family members. The girl goes on to say that she is not so sure whether her father is a person who plays by the rules or not. Then quickly she says, "I know my father is a person who knows the rules and plays by the rules."

This interview starts off with typical latency-age defenses, but develops thematic richness and depth even though the child is at an age at which fantasy life is thought to be more restricted along the dimension of control.

35

The example demonstrates that latency children are as capable of developing rich, deep themes as are Oedipal children, except that the direct access of the latency child to the underlying fantasy may be less facile. The healthy latency child may develop a rich, deep theme around the desire for control and regulation and how he or she has to contend with "those forces and people" who do not have similar inclinations.

Contrast the above example with a 9½-year-old girl who comes into the interview room and, instead of developing a rich, deep theme around rules and regulations stemming from a game of checkers, begins to play checkers, then switches to playing chess, and then switches to playing Monopoly, talking very little during any of these activities. This child, although concerned with rules, is more concerned with winning. She merely talks about the rules per se, sticking very much to the concrete details. There is almost no spontaneous elaboration about the implications of what she is doing. When she shows concern about "making the right moves" so that she will not lose her checkers, and the interviewer comments empathically that it's understandable that someone would want to make sure she did not lose any checkers, the child does not take off from this and talk about the theme of loss but continues talking about the checkers, never elaborating beyond the concrete level of the game. This girl, in contrast to the child in the above example, stays at a fairly superficial, fixed, and stereotyped level.

As indicated, the range and depth of thematic development provide a good initial picture of certain structural aspects of a child's internal life. The next subcategory, thematic sequence, is a source of clues to the nature of the child's particular concerns. Up to now, we have not talked about the content of the issues troubling a child. We have been discussing the form and structure of the personality—the theater in which the drama is portrayed. To see the drama, you must pay attention to the sequence of thematic productions. The drama's content may be murky, the issues disguised, but close examination of the sequence of themes will clarify what lies at the core—fear of closeness or separation, concern with various kinds of danger to one's body, rivalry with a younger sibling, etc.

For example, take a 6-year-old girl who takes all the family dolls and dramatically stuffs them into the toilet bowl. Then she gets scared and drops this play, thereby disrupting the thematic progress. She becomes hyperactive and starts punching the Bobo in a frenzied way. Following that, she calms down on her own and draws a family scene in which she is next to her father and her mother is far away. Then she smiles.

What does such a sequence suggest? She starts out with a theme of stuffing everyone down the toilet, from which you could hypothesize that she has either a wish to stuff or a fear that she will be stuffed down. Then there is anxiety and frenzied activity sufficient to create difficulty in getting her attention for a while, showing that probably the aggressive scene frightened her. Then she demonstrates that she is able to reorganize her capacity to communicate by calmly drawing a picture of the family, presumably the way she would like it to be, with her next to father. From this sequence, we can hypothesize concerns with overcrowding, (i.e., in the toilet bowl) in the family, aggression (some questions about what goes on in the bathroom), and a wish to be close to father in the family structure. Her ability to reorganize and return to the theme of family structure, reflecting her own (smiling) wish, shows her capacity for integration.

Consider the example of a latency-age boy. He is talking about school and says that the kids poke fun at him and that the teacher is not treating him fairly or being protective. The next theme concerns a brother or sister who gets more attention than he does at home. Then he stops talking to you and finds a gun to play with or starts shooting darts. After that he gets curious as to why he is there with you and wants to know something about you. You ask him what he has been told or what he thinks. He responds that you are a doctor who helps kids and you seem nice. You then comment that, in here, he feels that maybe he does not have to worry that someone will take advantage of him. In other words, via the above sequence of thematic development, this child is telling you that the world is unfair and that he hopes you are different but he is not sure. He wants you to reassure him.

Another child comes in placidly, sits down, and gives you a look that says, "OK, now entertain me." You wait a few minutes and then comment that it seems he just wants to sit and watch for a while, and you wonder what is going through his mind. That very passive child may eventually begin drawing explosions and cars crashing into one another. He may be too frightened to smash up the toy cars or take the toy gun and start shooting. Such a sequence yields a picture of a passive child with fears of explosive aggression.

The thematic sequence tells you not only what the core issues are but how they relate to one another. For example, a boy begins by shooting the gun and then looks scared; he takes a girl doll and looks under the dress, then throws it down. The child announces that he is "the strongest of all" and you comment that he sounds as if he is stronger than everyone else. He says,

"Yes, I am stronger than my little brother. I can beat him up. I can even beat up my mother and father." Here you see a child who starts off with aggression, shows concerns about the anatomy of girl dolls, and then makes himself powerful in order to deal with the fears and anxiety surrounding this aggression (i.e., a counterphobic style).

In the next sequence you may see this child becoming frantic, moving around the room and throwing things. You make a comment that he seems to be moving quickly and wants to throw everything around. Sometimes such a child then settles down and begins drawing pictures that express themes of yearning and early dependency. To return to the above example, once this child gets used to you and to the playroom, he may begin moving closer to you, wanting to involve you in the play. You get a subjective feeling of a strong yearning for close contact with someone. You may later sense, through drawings or other play, some feelings of emptiness. In summary, if you see aggression followed by dependency and yearning, you will have strong evidence that there is a significant relationship among these three issues.

Take one of the earlier examples, in which the child comes in, takes the gun, starts shooting, and then puts the baby doll in a safe place and begins doctoring and bandaging it. He then shows curiosity about what is going on behind the playroom door and develops a family drama about what his parents do in the bathroom and behind closed doors. This sequence gives a good picture of the nature of his concerns. It suggests, first, that he is concerned with his angry wishes, which are in conflict with his protective and caring wishes, and second, his curiosity about what his parents are doing behind closed doors. If, after talking about his parents, he begins talking about children getting sick and a cold he had the other day, and then wonders about going to the hospital and recalls his last visit to the doctor, we may see that his curiosity is also associated with fear of physical injury. His interest in what goes on behind closed doors and what goes on in the bathroom may be associated with fear about what can happen to him. From this example, we see how the thematic sequence gives us a ready and clearly interpretable picture of how concerns are related to each other in a child's mind.

Consider another example. A 7-year-old girl comes into the room and goes to the doll house, where she begins playing with the mother doll. She rounds up the family of dolls and uses a crayon to color over the dolls' faces. She then tries to detach the head of one of the dolls; not succeeding, she tries another doll and is able to rip off the head. There is a gleeful, somewhat eerie expression on her face: her eyes light up and she immediately grabs a ball and throws it against the wall, jumping around in a disorganized fashion. She runs over to the other side of the room and says she wants to play catch. She starts throwing the ball against the wall, narrowly missing some of the interviewer's favorite decorations. She continues this behavior, becoming more disorganized and fragmented. The interviewer comments on this behavior, which only makes it worse. Finally, the interviewer interrupts and suggests that they put the feelings into words rather than actions. When this tactic does not work, the interviewer has to go over and take away the ball lest all the furniture be broken.

This sequence suggests something fundamentally different than those discussed earlier. Here the girl shows her concern with aggressive themes by pulling off the head of a family member, but then she becomes disorganized and chaotic and cannot reorganize herself. She cannot return to the thematic area. We see aggression followed by disorganization. This not only tells us something about the child's concerns but also suggests that she is unable to handle these concerns, that they tend to disorganize her. She is not able to shift into a protective or caring mode, to change the theme on her own, or to demonstrate other maneuvers which would help her to deal with her frightening aggressive impulses. She was able to move away from the anxiety-laden situation only by abandoning herself to a general disorganization and impulsivity. Even though impulsivity in latency-age girls is less frequent than in boys of the same age, when it exists, it will emerge readily in the thematic sequence if the interviewer doesn't prematurely structure the situation.

As you learn to follow the sequence carefully, you will also be able to identify the developmental levels of the core conflicts. In other words, the dependency or the anger can exist at many levels. By examining the sequence closely, you will get some hunches as to whether the child's fears are age-appropriate.

For example, a 5-year-old may express an interest in your person that focuses on "what's hidden under your clothes," an age-appropriate curiosity. You may observe conflicts about this curiosity in the form of fear of body parts falling off (e.g., arms and legs of dolls falling off). In contrast, this same 5-year-old may show an interest in your person around themes of emotional hunger or basic security together with fears of global destruction and disorganization. Such themes are representative of developmentally earlier concerns.

As indicated, the thematic sequence provides clues about the nature of the child's concerns. The interviewer's goal is to follow the sequence of the child's thematic productions with minimal interference. Any comments should facilitate movement in the direction the child has chosen. They should *not* take the child in a new direction. The child's associations, one following another, will tell you his or her story better than any responses to your directions.

As discussed earlier in this chapter, you should note the sequences of events in the other categories as well (e.g., the sequence of the quality of relatedness to you, the sequence of the affects). When you combine your observations on the sequences of the content, the relatedness, and the affects, you have the material you need to make hypotheses about the child's conflicts. For example, from looking at the symmetry between the sequences of content and affect you can begin to get clues about the personality structure of a child. From the thematic development of an 8-year-old with an integrated ego structure, you may expect to learn something about the child's internal life and concerns; then ask yourself if these concerns are symmetrical to and integrated with the child's affects. The affects that emerge may point to anxiety and tensions around the disturbing issues. You might hypothesize, e.g., that the child is having some conflicts within the context of a basically intact ego structure.

Another aspect of thematic development that I have emphasized throughout this discussion is the assessment of age-appropriate relevance. Is the child concerned with the kinds of issues that you would expect, given your understanding of his or her background in terms of subculture, religion, and other relevant aspects? Is the child dealing with issues that seem above or below the age-appropriate level? Such questions will shed light on the content of the conflicts and how the child deals with them. The 13-year-old boy who talks about things that you expect to hear from a 7-year-old indicates his fear of entering adolescence and the degree of that fear. You frequently see early adolescents who are lingering in latency and, similarly, latency children who are behaving much more like Oedipal youngsters. For example, a 6-year-old boy may give you glimpses of 6-year-old behavior with competitive, assertive, or phallic themes. The child also displays negativistic belligerence and defiance, saying, "I won't do anything you want me to." He sits in the middle of the room and wants to be king of the place, ordering the therapist around. This boy is curious about things in the room, wants to know what is behind the doors, builds a few towers, but then quickly goes back to being negativistic and bossy, throwing things down and demanding that the therapist pick them up for him. Here we see movement between Oedipal themes and anal, pre-Oedipal ones. This kind of movement indicates that, although the child is working in the age-appropriate sphere, he must be frightened because he keeps retreating to earlier defensive positions.

On the other hand, the earlier example of the 5-year-old who starts shooting and then puts a baby doll in a safe place and begins bandaging it was rather typical of an Oedipal-age child. In his concerns, namely, competitive feelings toward a sibling, conflicts about aggressive and protective feelings, interest in his parents' bathroom and bedroom, and worries about the physical integrity of his own body, he is showing a number of age- and phase-appropriate Oedipal problems.

In summary, the aspects of thematic development discussed here include thematic organization, which focuses on the logical links or lack of them between the thematic elements; the themes' richness and depth, which concern the degree to which a child can develop a story before encountering restrictions or blocks that impede the unfolding of the story; thematic sequence, which contains clues to the child's concerns and core issues as well as to the kinds of defenses the child uses against the concerns; and the themes' age-appropriate relevance, which signals both the age level from which some of the child's conflicts derive and how the child handles the conflicts. Observations of these thematic elements will allow you to develop hypotheses about the child's characterological structure and central fears and conflicts.

## Subjective Reactions

The final category of observation concerns your own subjective reactions. There are two aspects to consider: the general feelings that the child evoked in you, and your fantasies during the interview. When you examine your reaction at the end of the interview, you want to know how the child made you feel—drained, elated, angry, frustrated, or what? Do you feel as though you conducted the interview poorly? Do you feel depressed about your own performance? Or do you feel as though you are the best diagnostician in the world?

For example, little girls sometimes tell a male interviewer everything he wants to know, making him feel masterful. After such a session you feel terrific, as if you had hardly even been working. The fact that you are feeling so great with this young girl may be a clue to the fact that she is dealing with significant Oedipal issues. On the other hand, if a male therapist is with a young boy who is being warm rather than competitive, and who makes the therapist feel good, the therapist's feelings may be a sign that the child is coping with some negative Oedipal issues affecting defensive structures.

Be very honest with yourself. What you are feeling is in some way related to the child and is separate from your own level of experience or competence. You will find that, no matter how experienced or inexperienced you are, with certain children you will feel competent and talented whereas with others you will feel inept and inadequate, as if you were tripping over yourself all the time. Such differences in your own reaction are significant: other things being equal, children who make you feel frustrated are quite different from children who make you feel good.

In addition to examining your general reaction, you also want to look at the sequence of specific fantasies that occur to you during the course of the diagnostic. If anything unusual comes to mind (e.g., highly personal memories or images), or if you find yourself not listening for a moment or two while attending your private associations, such a reaction may reflect your unique transference to this child. Later on, when you have time to reflect, discover what idiosyncrasy of yours started this line of thought. Then ask yourself why this thought came to you at this particular point in the interview. Regardless of what motivated this thought—be it hostility, exhibitionism, or whatever—use the information to understand why the child stimulated this response in you.

For example, too often we merely feel guilty if we find we have stopped listening. But if you feel yourself getting bored or sleepy, you should ask yourself, what is this child doing that elicits this reaction in me? The effect is immediately to make you more vigilant as you seek some insight into what the child is doing. In fact, he or she might be doing something that makes you anxious, and your defense is boredom or tiredness. In summary, your fleeting thoughts and subjective reactions are significant because they are part of the interactive matrix with a particular child at a given time.

## Summary

The categories I have been discussing in this chapter systematize and thereby stretch the potential implications of the observations you make when you meet a child in clinical interviews. As I explained at the start, multiple perspectives are necessary because behavior is so complicated and based on so many variables that the only way to get an understanding of it is to learn how to look at many dimensions simultaneously. Such an approach will keep you alert to the fact that any behavior can be based on a number of factors at once. I think it is an error to try to simplify prematurely by saying that a certain behavior belongs to only one category, such as the child's relatedness to the interviewer. In truth, this same behavior may be appropriately considered in several different frameworks.

Even a 3-minute capsule of a child's nonverbal behavior, observed from behind a one-way screen, for example, will yield a good initial picture of certain components of that child's personality and problems if you look at it from many different angles. What do the 3 minutes reveal about the child's physical and neurological integrity? Was the child coordinated? Does she show any gross motor incoordination? How is her fine motor coordination? What kind of activity did she engage in, and what was the activity level during those 3 minutes? Was the child hyperactive? Even if the child *was* hyperactive, you would want to observe more before making a hypothesis, for you do not know that the child always behaves that way.

You can also observe the emotional tone (e.g., the child seemed depressed, almost tearful), which is a clue to the child's overall mood. If, during the 3-minute interval, the child was clinging to the diagnostician, almost pleading for some kind of emotional contact and attention, that behavior may give you a sense of the degree of relatedness the child demands. In such a time-limited situation you will not have the child's thematic development to augment your observations, but you may experience a clear-cut subjective reaction that should be taken into account. Thus, even in a 3-minute segment, with only a few specific pieces of behavior to observe, you are able to develop hypotheses based on multiple perspectives.

# Chapter 3

# Chronological Age- and Phase-Appropriate Illustrations for Each Observational Category

This chapter will further illustrate the age- and phase-appropriate differences in the categories just described by means of a schematic chart. We will see that, for example, both the fine and the gross motor coordination of a 6- or 7-year-old are quite different from those of a 2- to 3-year-old. In a 2- or 3-year-old, coordination in gross motor capacities may already be developed, whereas some fine motor capacities will be just emerging (e.g., holding a pencil and drawing lines). By 7 or 8, in contrast, fine motor skills will be quite developed. With respect to style of relatedness, you would expect a 3-year-old to relate in a need-fulfilling manner, while you would expect a 7- or 8-year-old to show a more balanced capacity for partnership and sharing. In both instances, however, you would expect the capacity for emotional relatedness to be present.

In terms of mood, you might expect to see variations in the younger children depending on their immediate external circumstances. A shift from elation to sadness in the course of an hour would not raise concern. By 8 or 9 years old, in contrast, one would expect some stabilization of mood.

At the same time, the content of the mood—happy, sad, depressed, apprehensive, and so forth—would be independent of age and would be determined by the emerging personality structure of the youngster.

In terms of the organization, depth, variation, and (predominant) types of affect, age will be a determining factor. With a 2- or 3-year-old, we might see affects concerned with egocentric needs, jealousies, and so forth. By age 5 or 6 we expect a range of affects, with predominant types reflecting some degree of organization and depth around themes of jealousy and competition, as well as love and curiosity. By 8 or 9 years of age we expect to see still further development in the affective system and perhaps an emerging capacity for experiencing empathy, sadness, tenderness, and compassion together with the affects from earlier stages.

We may also expect differences depending on age in the organization, richness, depth, and sequence of themes. In 3- and 4-year-olds, for example, thematic organization will be limited: the child may dramatically shift themes without logical links. By age 5 and 6 we begin to see greater cohesion, although we are not surprised by "a theme seeming to jump out of left field." By 8 years of age, in contrast, we expect to see an organized elaboration of themes joined together by simple logical links.

Table 1 systematically illustrates age-appropriate differences in each category.

**Table 1** *A Developmental Approach to Observing Children:*
*Birth through Age 10*
A. FIRST YEAR

| OBSERVATIONAL CATEGORIES | 1ST YEAR |
| --- | --- |
| *1. Physical functioning: neurological, sensory, motor integrative*<br><br>Includes characteristic observations pertaining to the physical aspects of the child having to do with mental and psychological functioning, with special focus on the level of integration of the central nervous system, e.g., gross and fine motor coordination, perceptual-motor integration, emerging cognitive capacities. | Normal milestones, including turning toward stimulus, capacity to grab item in midline, sitting up, turning over, standing and eventually beginning to walk, clearer vocalizations, possibly a word or two (e.g., mama, dada), simple causal means-ends relationships with inanimate and animate world. Shows progress toward responding to social cues rather than internal sensations by 6 months, with increasing capacity to focus and concentrate as development progresses. |

**Table 1** *A Developmental Approach to Observing Children:*
*Birth through Age 10 (Continued)*
A. FIRST YEAR

| OBSERVATIONAL CATEGORIES | 1ST YEAR |
| --- | --- |
| *2. Pattern of relationships*<br><br>Includes characteristic style of relating or nonrelating (e.g., withdrawn, autistic), patterns of nonrelating, dyadic relating, capacity for group relating and sharing, egocentric styles of relating, etc. | General need for protection and comfort; multimodal interest in world evolves into highly individualized, interactive (reciprocal) affective relationship with primary caregivers. |
| *3. Overall mood or emotional tone*<br><br>Based on direct observation of specific emotions as well as themes or topics the child discusses. Characteristic patterns of this category may not be as clearly defined for each age group as those of the other categories. | Highly variable. Intimately related to internal states (e.g., hunger), and toward second half of first year also related to external social cues (parent can get even a hungry infant to smile). When internally comfortable, sense of interest and pleasure in world and in primary caregivers (e.g., drunken-sailor smile) should prevail. |
| *4. Affects*<br><br>Consideration of:<br><br>a. *Range and variety of affect:* the number of affects the child manifests: e.g., during early developmental phases range is limited or narrow; later the range is broader. Also includes characteristic types of affects: rage, jealousy, anger, empathy, love.<br><br>b. *Depth of affect expression:* substantive nature of affects manifested: shallow versus substantive, etc.<br><br>c. *Appropriateness of affect,* particularly in relationship to overall mood and content.<br><br>d. *Discriminative capacity of affects:* to what degree can the affects be highly discriminative of specific feeling states?<br><br>e. *Relationship of intensity of affect to stimulation or capacity for regulation of affect.* | Variation between indifference and excitement with world becomes more organized and under control of social interaction. Specific initial affects of pleasurable excitement and unpleasurable protest lead to more differentiated gradations of both pleasure and protest and apprehension (e.g., mild, moderate) toward end of first year. Affect system remains highly variable and is easily dominated by context. |

| OBSERVATIONAL CATEGORIES | 1ST YEAR |
|---|---|
| **5. *Anxieties and Fears*** | Anxiety is usually global and disorganizing. Underlying concern hypothesized to be related to themes of annihilation, loss of emerging self and world. |
| Best observed either in child's directly verbalized fears or indirectly through play. Anxiety in particular can be observed by disruptions in thematic development either during play or conversation. Level of anxiety can be indicated by nature of the disruption and themes which follow it, e.g., anxieties around fear of physical injury; or of more global, undifferentiated types such as fear of loss, world destruction, or fragmentation of one's inner self. | |
| **6. *Thematic Expression*** | Chaotic, seemingly purposeless, behavior related to internal cues evolves into simple social, purposeful, causal behavioral chains (e.g., mother smiles, baby reaches out with hand to elicit a similar response from mother) and simple reciprocal or contingent behavior. Capacity for organized, reciprocal interactions (e.g., mother smiles and baby smiles) to more complex chains of interaction toward end of first year (e.g., reaching out, holding object, and giving it to mother). Social interactions involve themes of pleasure, exploration, and protest. |
| Includes the capacity to express organized, developmentally appropriate, rich themes. How well can the child communicate his or her personality to another, either indirectly through play or directly through verbal communication? Clearly, some children develop such a capacity in time because their basic sense of trust in the world, their security about their own inner controls, and the availability of their fantasy life, enable them to communicate a rich feeling and content sense of themselves. Other children, by comparison, will be disorganized in their thematic expression (or very constricted, fragmented, impulsive, etc.). To further subdivide thematic expression, consider it from the following perspectives: | |

a. *Organization of thematic expression:* e.g., similar to organized or fragmented thinking.

b. *Depth and richness of thematic development.*

c. *Relevance in age-appropriate context:* How typical is content of themes to age-appropriate concerns?

d. *Thematic sequence.* This can be used in describing children at each age.

**Table 1** *A Developmental Approach to Observing Children: Birth through Age 10*

**B. SECOND YEAR**

| OBSERVATIONAL CATEGORIES | 2ND YEAR |
|---|---|
| *1. Physical functioning: neurological, sensory, motor integrative*<br><br>Includes characteristic observations pertaining to the physical aspects of the child having to do with mental and psychological functioning, with special focus on the level of integration of the central nervous system, e.g., gross and fine motor coordination, perceptual-motor integration, emerging cognitive capacities. | Normal milestones, including clumsy to coordinated walking and even running, climbing steps, etc. Fine motor capacities increasing (e.g., can scribble) and vocalizations becoming more distinct with capacity to name many objects and make needs known in two words; and near end of second year into third year, using sentences. Capacity for developing new behaviors from old ones (originality) and emerging capacity for symbolic activity (e.g., using words to describe self and others, play with dolls); variable capacity for concentration and self-regulation. |
| *2. Pattern of relationships*<br><br>Includes characteristic style of relating or nonrelating (e.g., withdrawn, autistic), patterns of nonrelating, dyadic relating, capacity for group relating and sharing, egocentric styles of relating, etc. | Dyadic relationship with primary caregivers evolves into a balance between need fulfillment (basic dependency) and emerging individuality, autonomy, initiative, and capacity for self-organization at the behavioral level (e.g., the toddler who goes to the refrigerator to get what he or she wants). Some negativism may be present. Issues of need and concerns with separation still paramount. |
| *3. Overall mood or emotional tone*<br><br>Based on direct observation of specific emotions as well as themes or topics the child discusses. Characteristic patterns of this category may not be as clearly defined for each age group as those of the other categories. | Also variable, but more organized and stable for longer periods of time. Sense of security, curiosity, and exploration should dominate over moods of emotional hunger, the tendency to cling, negativism, fear, and/or apprehension. A basic mood is beginning to emerge. |

| OBSERVATIONAL CATEGORIES | 2ND YEAR |
|---|---|

**4. Affects**

Consideration of:

a. *Range and variety of affect:* the number of affects the child manifests: e.g., during early developmental phases range is limited or narrow; later the range is broader. Also includes characteristic types of affects: rage, jealousy, anger, empathy, love.

b. *Depth of affect expression:* substantive nature of affects manifested: shallow versus substantive, etc.

c. *Appropriateness of affect,* particularly in relationship to overall mood and content.

d. *Discriminative capacity of affects:* to what degree can the affects be highly discriminative of specific feeling states?

e. *Relationship of intensity of affect to stimulation or capacity for regulation of affect.*

Affects of pleasure and displeasure become further differentiated. Observed are excited explorations, assertive pleasure, pleasure in discovery and in developing new behavior (e.g., new games). Capacity for organized demonstration of love (e.g., running up and hugging, smiling, and kissing parent—all together) and protest (e.g., turning away, crying, banging, and kicking—all together). Organized negativism (the no's) and clinging demandingness also present. Balance should be in direction of organized expressions of pleasure in discovery, initiative, and love. Comfort with family and apprehension with strangers may be more developed.

**5. Anxieties and Fears**

Best observed either in child's directly verbalized fears or indirectly through play. Anxiety in particular can be observed by disruptions in thematic development either during play or conversation. Level of anxiety can be indicated by nature of the disruption and themes which follow it, e.g., anxieties around fear of physical injury; or of more global, undifferentiated types such as fear of loss, world destruction, or fragmentation of one's inner self.

Anxiety related to loss of loved caretaker—potentially disorganizing.

Table 1 *A Developmental Approach to Observing Children:*
*Birth through Age 10 (Continued)*
B. SECOND YEAR

| OBSERVATIONAL CATEGORIES | 2ND YEAR |
|---|---|
| *6. Thematic Expression*<br><br>Includes the capacity to express organized, developmentally appropriate, rich themes. How well can child communicate his or her personality to another, either indirectly through play or directly through verbal communication? Clearly, some children develop such a capacity in time because their basic sense of trust in the world, their security about their own inner controls, and the availability of their fantasy life enable them to communicate a rich feeling and content sense of themselves. Other children, by comparison, will be disorganized in their thematic expression (or very constricted, fragmented, impulsive, etc.). To further subdivide thematic expression, consider it from the following perspectives:<br><br>   a. *Organization of thematic expression:* e.g., similar to organized or fragmented thinking.<br><br>   b. *Depth and richness of thematic development.*<br><br>   c. *Relevance in age-appropriate context.* How typical is content of themes to age-appropriate concerns?<br><br>   d. *Thematic sequence.* This can be used in describing children at each age. | Capacity for organization of behavior into complex causal chains (e.g., taking mother by hand to refrigerator and showing her desired food); initiative and originality at behavioral level as well as increased imitative identificatory behavior. At behavioral level child reflects themes of love and affiliation, curiosity, exploration and protest, anger, negativism and jealousy—all in organized modes (e.g., running to father and hugging and kissing him as one organized series; or turning away, throwing down toy, and screaming as another). Toward end of second year greater organization, possibly due to emerging capacities to symbolize and to *integrate* themes that reflect *polarities* of love and anger, passivity and activity, emerging, e.g., in one game—"The doll is bad, gets spanked, and then is hugged." |

**Table 1** *A Developmental Approach to Observing Children:*
*Birth through Age 10*
C. THIRD YEAR

| OBSERVATIONAL CATEGORIES | 3RD YEAR |
|---|---|
| *1. Physical functioning: neurological, sensory, motor integrative*<br><br>Includes characteristic observations pertaining to the physical aspects of the child having to do with mental and psychological functioning, with special focus on the level of integration of the central nervous system, e.g., gross and fine motor coordination, perceptual-motor integration, emerging cognitive capacities. | Very coordinated gross motor activity: running, walking up and down stairs without holding on, etc. Fine motor coordination more differentiated (e.g., can scribble circles, hold feeding utensils). Can name many objects, use personal pronouns and sentences to describe events, and make needs known. Symbolic capacity expanded as evidenced in wider fantasy life (e.g., dreams, fears, make-believe stories and people); capacity for concentration and self-regulation still variable but improving. |
| *2. Pattern of relationships*<br><br>Includes characteristic style of relating or nonrelating (e.g., withdrawn, autistic), patterns of nonrelating, dyadic relating, capacity for group relating and sharing, egocentric styles of relating, etc. | Relationships, though still dyadic and need-fulfilling, now become organized at a representational or symbolic level (i.e., a sense of self and other in terms of thoughts, memories, etc., is emerging) and permit use of fantasy. Balance between dependency and autonomy may shift for a brief time to the former. Power struggles and negativism may intermittently dominate relationship pattern. Dominant issues continue to be basic dependency and the need for security, and fear of separation. Capacity for more complex interactions since internal imagery can now be used (e.g., language or a doll used to represent needs in a complex game). |
| *3. Overall mood or emotional tone*<br><br>Based on direct observation of specific emotions as well as themes or topics the child discusses. Characteristic patterns of this category may not be as clearly defined for each age group as those of the other categories. | Initially may become quite variable (e.g., moody, fussy, and clinging behavior together with secure explorativeness), but then gradually stabilizes into even pattern organized around a basic sense of security and optimism, with capacity for excitement, negativism, passivity, tendency to cling, etc., present but not dominant. |

**Table 1** *A Developmental Approach to Observing Children:*
*Birth through Age 10 (Continued)*
C. THIRD YEAR

| OBSERVATIONAL CATEGORIES | 3RD YEAR |
|---|---|
| *4. Affects*<br><br>Consideration of:<br><br>a. *Range and variety of affect:* the number of affects the child manifests: e.g., during early developmental phases range is limited or narrow; later the range is broader. Also includes characteristic types of affects: rage, jealousy, anger, empathy, love.<br><br>b. *Depth of affect expression:* substantive nature of affects manifested: shallow versus substantive, etc.<br><br>c. *Appropriateness of affect,* particularly in relationship to overall mood and content.<br><br>d. *Discriminative capacity of affects:* to what degree can the affects be highly discriminative of specific feeling states?<br><br>e. *Relationship of intensity of affect to stimulation or capacity for regulation of affect.* | Affects now gradually have more "meaning" (representational or symbolic level). After possible initial instability in affect system (e.g., regressive, clinging anger and dependency), greater organization of affect system possible, with such complex affects of love, unhappiness, jealousy, and envy expressed at both preverbal and emerging verbal level. Affect system still easily influenced by somatic events (e.g., tiredness, hunger.) Affects still mostly at egocentric level ("What's in it for me"). |
| *5. Anxieties and Fears*<br><br>Best observed either in child's directly verbalized fears or indirectly through play. Anxiety in particular can be observed by disruptions in thematic development either during play or conversation. Level of anxiety can be indicated by nature of the disruption and themes which follow it, e.g., anxieties around fear of physical injury; or of more global, undifferentiated types such as fear of loss, world destruction, or fragmentation of one's inner self. List the characteristics and manifestations of anxieties and fears at different ages. | Anxiety related to loss of loved and depended-on person as well as loss of approval and acceptance. While still potentially disorganizing, anxiety can be better tolerated and may be coped with through alterations in mental imagery (fantasy) (e.g., "Mother will be back, she loves me"). |

*6. Thematic Expression*

Includes the capacity to express organized, developmentally appropriate, rich themes. How well can child communicate his or her personality to another, either indirectly through play or directly through verbal communication? Clearly, some children develop such a capacity in time because their basic sense of trust in the world, their security about their own inner controls, and the availability of their fantasy life, enable them to communicate a rich feeling and content sense of themselves. Other children, by comparison, will be disorganized in their thematic expression (or very constricted, fragmented, impulsive, etc.). To further subdivide thematic expression, consider it from the following perspectives:

 a. *Organization of thematic expression:* e.g., similar to organized or fragmented thinking.

 b. *Depth and richness of thematic development.*

 c. *Relevance in age-appropriate context:* How typical is content of themes to age-appropriate concerns?

 d. *Thematic sequence.* This can be used in describing children at each age.

Behavior remains organized as in second year and even more complex chains of interaction are possible. Now symbolic capacity, as evidenced by language and use of personal pronouns (I, you, etc.), and elaboration of fantasy through language and behavior (e.g., play in which child has one doll, mother another doll) emerge. In contrast to *organized* behavior, symbolic communication is initially fragmented (e.g., seemingly disconnected verbal communications). There is a gradual elaboration of experience (e.g., naming feelings and fears; repeating what is heard, first in fragmented form and then slowly in more organized modes). Themes involve repeating what is seen and heard, exploring inanimate and animate world with new symbolic capacities, and then using symbolic modes for emotional interaction. There is a vacillation between attempts at self-definition—through trying to be in "control," power struggles, negativism, and joyful and excited development of new behavior and thoughts (discovery at the symbolic level)—and regressive dependent interests (holding, clinging, etc.), which also have the element of "I'm in control," however. Improving capacity for self-control and responding to limits and structure at symbolic level. Interest in theme of power (e.g., rocket ships, powerful heros, pretending to be a monster and being scared of monsters) emerges toward end of third year.

## Table 1 *A Developmental Approach to Observing Children: Birth through Age 10*
### D. FOURTH YEAR

| OBSERVATIONAL CATEGORIES | 4TH YEAR |
|---|---|
| *1. Physical functioning: neurological, sensory, motor integrative*<br><br>Includes characteristic observations pertaining to the physical aspects of the child having to do with mental and psychological functioning, with special focus on the level of integration of the central nervous system, e.g., gross and fine motor coordination, perceptual-motor integration, emerging cognitive capacities. | Gross motor coordination continues to improve: child can run, jump, hop, throw a ball accurately, etc. Fine motor coordination improves, e.g., child can almost tie shoes, can draw circles, handles utensils very well. Can talk in full sentences with decent vocabulary in general interpersonal sense and to make needs known. Symbolic capacity not only expanded (e.g., complex play with dolls) but ability for reality orientation (distinguishing fantasy from reality) increasing; concentration and self-regulation possible with appropriate context and support. |
| *2. Pattern of relationships.*<br><br>Includes characteristic style of relating or nonrelating (e.g., withdrawn, autistic), patterns of nonrelating, dyadic relating, capacity for group relating and sharing, egocentric styles of relating, etc. | Relationship patterns becoming more complicated not only in content (language, symbolic modes) but in form, as dyadic patterns recede and capacities for dealing with triangular and other more complicated patterns emerge (e.g., rivalries, intrigues, secrets, two against one, jealousies, envy). Capacity for peer relationships increasing as well. Greater sense of security; capacity for separation and for carrying sense of the "other" inside relatively well established by end of fourth year. Anger and other strong feelings do not compromise secure capacity for separation. Capacity for true (not simply need-fulfilling) intimacy in relationships emerging more fully. |
| *3. Overall mood or emotional tone*<br><br>Based on direct observation of specific emotions as well as themes or topics the child discusses. Characteristic patterns of this category may not be as clearly defined for each age group as those of the other categories. | Mood stabilizes further and organizes complex feelings; less extreme reactions to frustration (e.g., having to delay). Basic attitude toward self and world conveyed in organized mood, which optimally reflects security in psychological and bodily self and curious expansive interest with periodic excitement in family, peers, and the world. Sadness, insecurity, negativism receding in importance. |

| OBSERVATIONAL CATEGORIES | 4TH YEAR |
|---|---|

*4. Affects*

Consideration of:

a. *Range and variety of affect:* the number of affects the child manifests: e.g., during early developmental phases range is limited or narrow; later the range is broader. Also includes characteristic types of affects: rage, jealousy, anger, empathy, love.

b. *Depth of affect expression:* Substantive nature of affects manifested: shallow versus substantive, etc.

c. *Appropriateness of affect,* particularly in relationship to overall mood and content.

d. *Discriminative capacity of affects:* to what degree can the affects be highly discriminative of specific feeling states?

e. *Relationship of intensity of affect to stimulation or capacity for regulation of affect.*

Pride and joy in psychological and bodily self further emerge. Increased interest in power; affects of shame and humiliation become dominant. Increased feelings of jealousy and envy; more differentiated sadistic and masochistic trends. Emerging capacity for sharing and concern for others. Empathy and tenderness hinted at. Affect system well-organized, showing large number of affect states of the emerging sense of self.

*5. Anxieties and Fears*

Best observed either in child's directly verbalized fears or indirectly through play. Anxiety in particular can be observed by disruptions in thematic development either during play or conversation. Level of anxiety can be indicated by nature of the disruption and themes which follow it, e.g., anxieties around fear of physical injury; or of more global, undifferentiated types such as fear of loss, world destruction, or fragmentation of one's inner self.

Anxiety over loss of loved person's approval and bodily injury sometimes disruptive, but usually not.

55

**Table 1** *A Developmental Approach to Observing Children: Birth through Age 10 (Continued)*

D. FOURTH YEAR

| OBSERVATIONAL CATEGORIES | 4TH YEAR |
| --- | --- |
| *6. Thematic Expression*<br><br>Includes the capacity to express organized, developmentally appropriate, rich themes. How well can child communicate his or her personality to another, either indirectly through play or directly through verbal communication? Clearly, some children develop such a capacity in time because their basic sense of trust in the world, their security about their own inner controls, and the availability of their fantasy life enable them to communicate a rich feeling and content sense of themselves. Other children, by comparison, will be disorganized in their thematic expression (or very constricted, fragmented, impulsive, etc.). To further subdivide thematic expression, consider it from the following perspectives:<br><br>a. *Organization of thematic expression:* e.g., similar to organized or fragmented thinking.<br><br>b. *Depth and richness of thematic development.*<br><br>c. *Relevance in age-appropriate context.* How typical is content of themes to age-appropriate concerns?<br><br>d. *Thematic sequence.* This can be used in describing children at each age. | Thematic organization at behavioral level continues in a richer, more complex fashion. Now, however, complex themes at a symbolic level are also becoming organized compared to fragmentation of third year (e.g., organized verbal elaboration of fantasy now possible in the reporting of a dream: "A monster came in and was going to attack me, but then I punched him in the nose . . ." and in symbolic play: building a fort to protect dolls from the various monsters; having a "tea party," cooking various foods and serving guests). Some vacillation between these organized themes and fragmented ones, but indications of rich, organized inner life present. Content of themes a product of inner fantasy life. Capacity for reality orientation present as well—"that's just make-believe." Tendency is to be swept away by fantasy for short periods of time. In *circumscribed areas* fantasy may dominate reality over long periods, for example, in fears around going to sleep, and with imaginary friends. Themes around both aggression- and pleasure-derived power and interest in and fear of the body dominate, together with curiosity, a sense of discovery, feelings of pride, admiration of self and others, and emerging concerns with shame. Also present are concerns with security, fears of loss of love and separation, and remnants of power struggles and issues of control. |

**Table 1** *A Developmental Approach to Observing Children:*
*Birth through Age 10*
E. FIFTH AND SIXTH YEARS

| OBSERVATIONAL CATEGORIES | 5TH AND 6TH YEARS |
|---|---|
| *1. Physical functioning: neurological, sensory, motor integrative*<br><br>Includes characteristic observations pertaining to the physical aspects of the child having to do with mental and psychological functioning, with special focus on the level of integration of the central nervous system, e.g., gross and fine motor coordination, perceptual-motor integration, emerging cognitive capacities. | Gross motor coordination improves, as evidenced by more accurate throwing, rhythmic jumping (rope), kicking (e.g., football). Fine motor coordination improves, e.g., ties shoes; writes letters; draws circles, squares, and triangles; talks in full, complex sentences; begins to demonstrate capacity to present ideas. Originality. Can begin to conceptualize simple reciprocal and inverse relationships; capacity for self-regulation and concentration improving, but still subject to context and support. |
| *2. Pattern of relationships*<br><br>Includes characteristic style of relating or nonrelating (e.g., withdrawn, autistic), patterns of nonrelating, dyadic relating, capacity for group relating and sharing, egocentric styles of relating, etc. | Complex triangular modes dominate family life as relationships take on "soap opera" dimensions of intrigue, rivalry, alliances, etc. Simple need-fulfilling two-person relationships pattern no longer dominant. Capacity to relate comfortably with others—peers, teachers, etc. Growing capacity for separation, internal security; ability to carry a sense of "self" and "other" inside not only well established but not easily compromised by separations or strong affects. |
| *3. Overall mood or emotional tone*<br><br>Based on direct observation of specific emotions as well as themes or topics the child discusses. Characteristic patterns of this category may not be as clearly defined for each age group as those of the other categories. | Stable, organized mood characterized by expressiveness and curiosity. Variations in affect (e.g., fearfulness, inhibition, unwillingness to compromise) but overall organization and stability of mood. |

**Table 1** *A Developmental Approach to Observing Children:*
*Birth through Age 10 (Continued)*
E. FIFTH AND SIXTH YEARS

| OBSERVATIONAL CATEGORIES | 5TH AND 6TH YEARS |
| --- | --- |
| *4. Affects*<br><br>Consideration of:<br><br>a. *Range and variety of affect:* the number of affects the child manifests: e.g., during early developmental phases range is limited or narrow; later the range is broader. Also includes characteristic types of affects: rage, jealousy, anger, empathy, love.<br><br>b. *Depth of affect expression:* substantive nature of affects manifested: shallow versus substantive, etc.<br><br>c. *Appropriateness of affect,* particularly in relationship to overall mood and content.<br><br>d. *Discriminative capacity of affects:* to what degree can the affects be highly discriminative of specific feeling states?<br><br>e. *Relationship of intensity of affect to stimulation or capacity for regulation of affect.* | Many individual affects in relatively stable pattern: expansiveness, curiosity, pride, gleeful excitement related to discovery of bodily self and family patterns; balanced with coyness, shyness, fearfulness, jealousy, and envy. Shame and humiliation still dominant. Capacity for empathy and love developed, but fragile and easily lost if competitive or jealous strivings are on the upsurge. |
| *5. Anxieties and Fears*<br><br>Best observed either in child's directly verbalized fears or indirectly through play. Anxiety in particular can be observed by disruptions in thematic development either during play or conversation. Level of anxiety can be indicated by nature of the disruption and themes which follow it, e.g., anxieties around fear of physical injury; or of more global, undifferentiated types such as fear of loss, world destruction, or fragmentation of one's inner self. | Anxiety and fears related to bodily injury and loss of respect, love, and emerging self-esteem; self-esteem may vacillate between extremes. Guilt feelings possible. |

OBSERVATIONAL CATEGORIES

*6. Thematic Expression*

Includes the capacity to express organized, developmentally appropriate, rich themes. How well can child communicate his or her personality to another, either indirectly through play or directly through verbal communication? Clearly, some children develop such a capacity in time because their basic sense of trust in the world, their security about their own inner controls, and the availability of their fantasy life enable them to communicate a rich feeling and content sense of themselves. Other children, by comparison, will be disorganized in their thematic expression (or very constricted, fragmented, impulsive, etc.). To further subdivide thematic expression, consider it from the following perspectives:

a. *Organization of thematic expression:* e.g., similar to organized or fragmented thinking.

b. *Depth and richness of thematic development.*

c. *Relevance in age-appropriate context.* How typical is content of themes to age-appropriate concerns?

d. *Thematic sequence.* This can be used in describing children at each age.

5TH AND 6TH YEARS

Extremely rich, organized, complex, symbolic thematic capacity with occasional fragmentation. While capable of being swept away by the fantasy, reality orientation well established. "That's not real" except at times in certain circumscribed areas around fears, etc. Content of themes represent rich, complex interest in major issues of the world: sex, aggression, power, curiosity, discovery, emerging morality, etc. Polarities of love, pleasure, and aggression should be present and integrated into complex, rich themes (e.g., game where child first takes care of sibling in a loving fashion, later becomes an attacking monster, and then becomes concerned with retaliation). For the first time, triangular patterns in relationships emerge in thematic expression—feeling left out, wishing to leave someone else out, game or fantasy of getting rid of "other" person in triangle, etc. Slight shift from interests in power and one's own body and how it compares to others', to real curiosity about others and their bodies and what goes on "behind closed doors." Fear of bodily injury takes over, although earlier fears of loss of approval and separation are present. Emerging fear of loss of own self-esteem now possible.

**Table 1** *A Developmental Approach to Observing Children:*
*Birth through Age 10*
F. SEVENTH AND EIGHTH YEARS

| OBSERVATIONAL CATEGORIES | 7TH AND 8TH YEARS |
| --- | --- |
| *1. Physical functioning: neurological, sensory, motor integrative*<br><br>Includes characteristic observations pertaining to the physical aspects of the child having to do with mental and psychological functioning, with special focus on the level of integration of the central nervous system, e.g., gross and fine motor coordination, perceptual-motor integration, emerging cognitive capacities. | Gross motor coordination improves even further as child can now do most activities: running, jumping, hopping, skipping, throwing, etc. Fine motor coordination improves, as evidenced by being able to write more fluently in script, improved drawing, etc. Language used more and more in complete sentences to present wishes, needs, and fantasies, as well as logical ideas of a simple nature, oriented toward making orderly sense of the world. Capacity for self-regulation, following rules, and concentrating established. |
| *2. Pattern of relationships*<br><br>Includes characteristic style of relating or nonrelating (e.g., withdrawn, autistic), patterns of nonrelating, dyadic relating, capacity for group relating and sharing, egocentric styles of relating, etc. | Interest in relationships outside family groups (e.g., peers) and capacity for organized orderly patterns of relating to others (e.g., games with rules) emerge. Some aspects of earlier patterns still present, however (e.g., power struggles, passive helplessness, family intrigues, rivalries, triangles). Capacity for "buddy" and intimacy with a few "best" friends emerging more fully. |
| *3. Overall mood or emotional tone*<br><br>Based on direct observation of specific emotions as well as themes or topics the child discusses. Characteristic patterns of this category may not be as clearly defined for each age group as those of the other categories. | Stable, organized mood characterized by emerging realistic appraisal of self, others, and world, and by emerging ideals. Expansive curiosity balanced with more sober, orderly approach. |

| OBSERVATIONAL CATEGORIES | 7TH AND 8TH YEARS |
|---|---|

*4. Affects*

Consideration of:

a. *Range and variety of affect:* the number of affects the child manifests: e.g., during early developmental phases range is limited or narrow; later the range is broader. Also includes characteristic types of affects: rage, jealousy, anger, empathy, love.

b. *Depth of affect expression:* substantive nature of affects manifested: shallow versus substantive, etc.

c. *Appropriateness of affect,* particularly in relationship to overall mood and content.

d. *Discriminative capacity of affects:* to what degree can the affects be highly discriminative of specific feeling states?

e. *Relationship of intensity of affect to stimulation or capacity for regulation of affect.*

Concern for others, empathy, worry, and pleasure in approval, over success, and over mastery (self-esteem) emerge and operate in balance with the expansive and competitive affects described above. Less variation in specific affects, though large number of affects still possible. Some instability between attempts to keep self in order and on right track (e.g., affects of self-praise, self-esteem) and earlier expansive and rivalrous affects. At times, earlier affects of primitive envy, negativism, and egocentric emotional hunger pervade.

*5. Anxieties and Fears*

Best observed either in child's directly verbalized fears or indirectly through play. Anxiety in particular can be observed by disruptions in thematic development either during play or conversation. Level of anxiety can be indicated by nature of the disruption and themes which follow it, e.g., anxieties around fear of physical injury; or of more global, undifferentiated types such as fear of loss, world destruction, or fragmentation of one's inner self.

Anxiety is occasionally disruptive, usually serves a signal function and can be dealt with via shift in fantasy or change in meanings (e.g., reaction formations).

61

**Table 1** *A Developmental Approach to Observing Children:*
*Birth through Age 10 (Continued)*
F. SEVENTH AND EIGHTH YEARS

| OBSERVATIONAL CATEGORIES | 7TH AND 8TH YEARS |
| --- | --- |
| *6. Thematic Expression*<br><br>Includes the capacity to express organized, developmentally appropriate, rich themes. How well can child communicate his or her personality to another, either indirectly through play or directly through verbal communication? Clearly, some children develop such a capacity in time because their basic sense of trust in the world, their security about their own inner controls, and the availability of their fantasy life enable them to communicate a rich feeling and content sense of themselves. Other children, by comparison, will be disorganized in their thematic expression (or very constricted, fragmented, impulsive, etc.). To further subdivide thematic expression, consider it from the following perspectives:<br><br>a. *Organization of thematic expression:* e.g., similar to organized or fragmented thinking.<br><br>b. *Depth and richness of thematic development.*<br><br>c. *Relevance in age-appropriate context.* How typical is content of themes to age-appropriate concerns?<br><br>d. *Thematic sequence.* This can be used in describing children at each age. | Relatively rich, organized thematic development with perhaps slightly less richness or breadth than in 5- to 6-year-old period, but more organized with less fragmentation. Less emphasis now on expanding interest in world, triangles, intrigues, the human body, what goes on behind closed doors, and various aggressive themes (monsters, attacking, etc.); more emphasis on containing these interests (e.g., "I'm not interested in what's going on behind the door, let me look and I'll show you I'm not interested"). In sense of polarities, there is a slight shift from pleasurable pursuits toward themes of control but balance should still be present. Interest in "roles" (what I am—"a football player," etc.) emerging as more dominant. Activity and assertion should be better modulated (e.g., regulates self and follows instructions). Occasional passive compliance may be present. Sense of morality (what's right and wrong) emerging but still unstable. Concern with rules and structure emerging; relatively greater interest in peers and the group, and slightly diminished interest in the family and adults. |

**Table 1** *A Developmental Approach to Observing Children:*
*Birth through Age 10*

**G. NINTH AND TENTH YEARS**

| OBSERVATIONAL CATEGORIES | 9TH AND 10TH YEARS |
| --- | --- |
| *1. Physical functioning: neurological, sensory, motor integrative*<br><br>Includes characteristic observations pertaining to the physical aspects of the child having to do with mental and psychological functioning, with special focus on the level of integration of the central nervous system, e.g., gross and fine motor coordination, perceptual-motor integration, emerging cognitive capacities. | Greater muscle strength enhances gross motor coordination; gradual further improvement in all areas, with the capacity for complex activities (e.g., basketball, football, tennis). New learning more established. Fine motor coordination also improves, with more fluid writing and the capacity to take things apart (e.g., with screwdriver) skillfully. Language now used to express complex ideas with relationships among a number of elements, e.g., "I did this because he did that, and he did that because she made him." Tendency for logical exploration to dominate fantasy; greater sense of morality; increased interest in rules and orderliness; increased capacity for self-regulation; well-established ability to concentrate. |
| *2. Pattern of relationships*<br><br>Includes characteristic style of relating or nonrelating (e.g., withdrawn, autistic), patterns of nonrelating, dyadic relating, capacity for group relating and sharing, egocentric styles of relating, etc. | Family relationships and friendships quite organized around role models (e.g., simplified adult stereotypes). Relaxed capacity for integrating and enjoying family, peer, teacher and other adult relationships. Special relationship with same-sex parent as role model, with only hints of earlier levels (e.g., triangles, power struggles, passive manipulation). Preparation for adolescent styles of relating emerging, with special patterns of relating to same- and opposite-sex peers. Capacity for *long-term* relationships with family, peers, and friends—including "best friend(s)." |
| *3. Overall mood or emotional tone*<br><br>Based on direct observation of specific emotions as well as themes or topics the child discusses. Characteristic patterns of this category may not be as clearly defined for each age group as those of the other categories. | Stability, depth, and organization of mood further developed, as evidenced by capacity to deal with frustration, complex interpersonal relationships, etc., with sense of curiosity and *realistic* optimism (which is gradually replacing expansiveness). Depression, negativism, passive helplessness, and withdrawn moods should only emerge intermittently (e.g., in appropriate circumstances of stress). |

63

**Table 1** *A Developmental Approach to Observing Children:*
*Birth through Age 10 (Continued)*
G. NINTH AND TENTH YEARS

| OBSERVATIONAL CATEGORIES | 9TH AND 10TH YEARS |
| --- | --- |
| *4. Affects*<br><br>Consideration of:<br><br>a. *Range and variety of affect:* the number of affects the child manifests: e.g., during early developmental phases range is limited or narrow; later the range is broader. Also includes characteristic types of affects: rage, jealousy, anger, empathy, love.<br><br>b. *Depth of affect expression:* substantive nature of affects manifested: shallow versus substantive, etc.<br><br>c. *Appropriateness of affect,* particularly in relationship to overall mood and content.<br><br>d. *Discriminative capacity of affects:* to what degree can the affects be highly discriminative of specific feeling states?<br><br>e. *Relationship of intensity of affect to stimulation or capacity for regulation of affect.* | Well-developed capacity for empathy, love, compassion, sharing, and emerging capacity for sadness and loss in context of concrete rules. Internal self-esteem very important. Feelings of guilt and internalized fears present. Expansive lust, hunger, and jealousy in background. New affects around sexual differences beginning to emerge (e.g., excitement and shyness in relation to sexual themes). |
| *5. Anxieties and Fears*<br><br>Best observed either in child's directly verbalized fears or indirectly through play. Anxiety in particular can be observed by disruptions in thematic development either during play or conversation. Level of anxiety can be indicated by nature of the disruption and themes which follow it, e.g., anxieties around fear of physical injury; or of more global, undifferentiated types such as fear of loss, world destruction, or fragmentation of one's inner self. | Anxiety related to internalized conflicts generally not disruptive; may be disphoric and/or serve a signal function and lead to change in behavior, interpretation of events, or more sophisticated changes in meanings and fantasies (e.g., rationalizations). |

| OBSERVATIONAL CATEGORIES | 9TH AND 10TH YEARS |
|---|---|

*6. Thematic Expression*

Includes the capacity to express organized, developmentally appropriate, rich themes. How well can child communicate his or her personality to another, either indirectly through play or directly through verbal communication? Clearly, some children develop such a capacity in time because their basic sense of trust in the world, their security about their own inner controls, and the availability of their fantasy life enable them to communicate a rich feeling and content sense of themselves. Other children, by comparison, will be disorganized in their thematic expression, (or very constricted, fragmented, impulsive, etc.). To further subdivide thematic expression, consider it from the following perspectives:

a. *Organization of thematic expression:* e.g., similar to organized or fragmented thinking.

b. *Depth and richness of thematic development.*

c. *Relevance in age-appropriate context.* How typical is content of themes to age-appropriate concerns?

d. *Thematic sequence.* This can be used in describing children at each age.

Thematic capacity quite well-organized, e.g., capable of relating organized story about the robbers who are caught by the policemen in great detail, with elaborations of the robbers' plans and how the policemen fooled them. Stories of football games or parties where adult roles are imitated are also presented in a detailed, organized manner. Little or no fragmentation as more and more interrelated detail can be organized. Some of the emotional richness and complexity of the 5- to 6-year-old phase relinquished for greater interest in themes around control, rules, organization, and higher-level domination-submission themes. The new interest in "roles" and "what I will be" and differences between boys and girls emerging. Variable interest in talking both with peers and, somewhat sheepishly, with adults about sex (e.g., dirty jokes with giggling) in anticipation of adolescence. Concerns with self-regard and how others regard one are also prominent. Internal morality relatively well established in concrete "black and white" sense, but still easy to rationalize breaking the rules. In fact, along with greater concern with right and wrong is more sophisticated capacity for rationalizing and getting around the rules. Self-control and capacity to follow instructions should be quite well established, however.

65

# Chapter 4

# Clinical Illustrations of
# Interviews with Children

The clinical materials presented below—interview patterns developed by 11 young children—were constructed from brief process notes that I made after each interview. The reader may wish to read these illustrative examples and then attempt to organize the data according to the categories outlined earlier. A first-level clinical inference may then be attempted in terms of describing whether each category of functioning is at the appropriate age level or below it. In a subsequent chapter on making clinical judgments, the elaboration of these inferences into clinical hypotheses will be discussed.

## Case 1

*Interview*

Doug was a well-groomed, average-sized boy of 8½ years. He was sitting on a chair next to his mother in the waiting room, doodling on a pad that he had brought with him. He looked up with a blank expression when I asked him to join me, and readily came into the office with me. He had a somewhat sober, perhaps even sad look about him. He made ready eye contact, however, was well-coordinated, and walked in an easygoing fashion. He sat on the couch and, without saying a word, scribbled on his pad. His fine motor coordination looked good; he was able to manipulate the pen well. He was right-handed.

During a brief, mildly uncomfortable pause, as I waited to see if he would begin communication, it appeared that he was almost frozen with silence. He just sat there. After I saw that he was not about to break the silence, I commented that he liked to draw and doodle. He quickly responded that it was OK to doodle, but he had no strong feelings about it one way or another. I then sat down next to him and noticed that he was drawing a cartoon figure. The profiled face had a square nose and a big mouth, with the word "Hi" coming out of it. The figure had a trunk but no legs. I commented that Doug seemed to like to draw cartoons; he quickly replied that it was his brother who really liked to draw cartoons.

Doug pointed out that he ran errands, going to the store for groceries and the like, and then elaborated about how he had started a little business. His family lived in an apartment and for a quarter he would do errands for other families in the building. At this point in the interview he started getting affectively excited and emotionally involved. "They give me big tips," he said. "I got a dollar today for going shopping for a lady." He then related with pleasure and pride that he had made $30 in the last month, and that when he made $30 more, he would have $560 in the bank and then he would have "enough" money.

I was curious about what the money was for and what he meant by "enough" money. He said, "Enough is for the future, in case of an emergency." I said, "There are a lot of different kinds of emergencies." (It is best not to ask questions of children—e.g., "What kind of an emergency are you worried about?" It is more constructive simply to comment empathically about their concerns.) In response to my remark, Doug said only that it is always good to have money because there are all kinds of emergencies. He did not develop the theme more specifically, but did make side comments about inflation, world conditions, and the selling of airplanes to Arabs.

As he talked to me, Doug became more relaxed and looked more often in my direction. Although his voice reflected a degree of sadness and a narrow affective range, he showed generally increasing interest, some pleasure, and particularly some pride as he talked about his business interest and making money for the future. His verbal communication was well organized; that is, he chose a topic and discussed it without getting lost or going off on a tangent. He illustrated his topic—how important it was to be a good businessman—with pertinent examples.

The money theme, in various modes, permeated the interview. It was not good, he told me, to "buy lots of toys now, because it is better to have money for later." He told me about schoolmates who spent all their money on toys and said that he did not do that. Upon inquiry he told me that he learned this from his parents, that his whole family was very concerned with "saving money." (The boy's father is an extraordinarily successful author.)

He then told me about "lazy bums who live in the street and don't work, and don't have money or a place to sleep." I commented that this sounded kind of sad and unfortunate. He replied that he was not sympathetic, that they were lazy and it was their problem that they could not earn money. He seemed annoyed at their laziness. He also said that these people may be "stupid" as well as lazy, and that they do not take care of themselves. He went on with the theme of people who do not take care of themselves or plan for the future. Whenever I commented that he seemed to be just the opposite, he appeared very pleased and further elaborated about these lazy people. He told me spontaneously what he was worried would happen: something to do with an emergency and with why he was not like these lazy people. I was curious what he thought these lazy people who lie in the street were like. I began, "Gee, there are all kinds of lazy people who don't take care of themselves," and continued free-associating for half a minute about "lazy bums." Then he told me, "Well, a lot of them are 'robbers,' these 'lazy bums.' "

During this time he made relatively good eye contact and affective engagement. He was unusual in that he talked a blue streak and did not explore the room, staying focused on the issues of protecting oneself from future emergencies and lazy bums.

Next he talked about robbers coming into the house and how his little brother (who is 2½ years old) would not know what to do and would get hurt. He then abruptly returned to the topic of future emergencies and began to clarify what he meant by emergencies. He spoke of people getting sick, having cancer and other illnesses that people die from, and said that you never know when you are going to die. Then he talked briefly about his older brother and what his older brother is better at than he is, and about his younger brother, saying that the latter was a pest. However, he added that he was learning to adjust to the younger brother and did not really want to get rid of him. He returned to the subject of physical illness and became preoccupied with it. He associated in a free-wheeling and unusually open manner, almost like someone lying on the couch. There was no sense of his being guarded about what he was saying. His affect during these disclosures was reasonably engaging with a mildly hungry quality.

Near the end of the session he expressed a worry from out of the blue. He asked if his older brother would know what we were talking about; that is, if the session was tape-recorded, could his brother find out? He quickly changed his mind about this, saying, "No, that's silly, that's not possible"; then he wondered if we could do things together, play basketball or tennis.

When I asked about his family, he became very anxious. He mentioned something about the things he liked to do with his father, such as play ball. (I knew that his father had a serious heart disease.) When discussing his activities with father, Doug got to the issue of his father's physical limitations and became acutely anxious, freezing for a second and then changing the subject very quickly. I tried to bring him back to the subject by commenting, "Gee, sometimes it's scary to talk about people not being able to do things." He pretended not to have heard and started bouncing a ball.

The interview ended with his wanting me to play tennis and basketball with him. He was quite intent on playing a game, almost insisting on an answer. He showed a lot of longing and emotional hunger. I felt as though he wanted to take me home to be his friend.

COMMENTS

Doug's physical and neurological functioning seemed intact. His mood conveyed an underlying sadness, longing, and depression, in contrast to the happy assertiveness one would expect of an 8-year-old. He projected an overall relatedness that was intense and emotionally hungry in style. There was a clear capacity for human relationships, but it had an affect-hungry quality to it rather than the sharing we would ordinarily expect in an 8-year-old. The affect system appeared organized but lacked depth and variety. I observed a general apprehension studded with preoccupations about guarding against future emergencies and fear of being hurt, robbed, and ill. I did not see a range of affects—from empathy and love to competitive anger, for example. Rather, the affect range was constricted around fearful concerns and some competitive feelings toward siblings.

During the course of the interview, I saw highly competent, age-appropriate thematic organization (though not content) except on the subject of his father's physical limitations, which provoked an abrupt switch in topic. Near the end of the interview, however, the organization loosened remarkably; although he kept to the topic, he seemed almost to be free-associating like an adult in psychoanalysis. His concern that his brother might find out what he was saying demonstrated a breakthrough of seemingly unrelated fantasy into his reality. This breakthrough, together with his hungry style of relatedness, raises a question about the integrity of his personality structure. That this structure is below the age-appropriate level would be a hypothesis worth examining.

In terms of thematic depth and richness, although I saw that this child was able to communicate a number of his concerns vividly, these concerns were few. That he was able to share what was on his mind is an important asset, yet he made no mention of school, mastery, friendships, or other common age-appropriate concerns.

The thematic sequence gives us important clues to his conflicts. His concern with doing things right, followed by his worry that robbers might take his brother, fear of the future, and fear of bodily injury, dramatize how close to the surface many of his conflicts are. The sequence shows him to be an emotionally hungry child who feels the need for more physical warmth and closeness from human beings, and who worries about how he can satisfy these needs.

My subjective feeling toward Doug was initially positive. I thought him an interesting and talkative child capable of making fairly good contact. I felt that he cared for and liked me. Before long, however, I felt a sense of apprehension, thinking that this child was going to be very demanding; I was not sure that I wanted to get close to him. I thought, "This child wants more than I may want to give." My feelings ranged from being elated to feeling trapped. I had no noteworthy idiosyncratic fantasies during that hour.

## Case 2

*Interview*

Harold, a 7½-year-old, was in the waiting room with his mother when I first saw him. Most notable was his running back and forth in a seemingly provocative way, teasing his mother. When she insisted that he sit down for fear that he would break something, he sat fidgeting in a chair for about 30 seconds, then got up and started throwing a little ball that he had brought. He disregarded his mother's continuing commands that he return to his seat.

I introduced myself to Harold and he willingly came into the playroom, where he continued throwing his ball. Twice the ball came close to me, and my immediate subjective reaction concerned the degree to which Harold was aiming the ball at me. He spoke in a clear but nasal voice with a slight lisp. His gross motor coordination, which was amply displayed since he was continually in motion, seemed age-appropriate. Later on during the interview, when he showed me how he could make letters, I noted that his fine motor coordination seemed less than age-appropriate. His letters were indistinct; he often failed to close circles and missed many connections between loops and lines.

While moving around the room throwing his ball, Harold made good eye contact with me and kept coming to and fro in a playful manner, although he did not engage me in his ball-throwing game. He looked around the entire room and at the various toys. He quickly picked out a gun, threw the ball up, and pretended to shoot it. He commented, "This is fun," but again did not try to involve me. He continued to throw the ball and shoot it with the gun for a few minutes. Then he spotted some racing cars, which he instantly grabbed and started zooming along the floor, one car after the other. He seemed to lack the patience or capacity to roll them on their wheels, but rather shoved them almost as though to throw them, seeing which one would go farthest and fastest. Around this time I commented that he was interested in movement and speed as reflected in the cars and in his running around. Ignoring my comment, he continued to race the cars. He did not look in my direction while I was talking, nor did he respond, although he did talk to his cars, saying, "Speedo, speedo, you'll beat the other one."

He spotted ropes hanging from the drapes in the room and began pulling on them and spinning them around. I had to intercede for fear that he would pull the ropes off. With a flirtatious grin on his face, he taunted and teased me that he would not stop. After a while, however, he sensed that my patience was growing thin and, when I told him to stop in a loud firm voice, he took three more seemingly playful swipes and then went back to zooming his racing cars. He then went over to a big Bobo doll in the corner of the room and began boxing with it, announcing, "I can beat up anyone, I am Superman." He was swinging at the Bobo in a somewhat chaotic fashion and I suggested, "Superman can do lots of things. What are all the things that you can do that are like Superman?" For the first time he chose to engage me. He said, "I'm strong, I can beat up all the kids at school. I can beat up my brother" (who is younger than he), and he continued hitting the Bobo. I commented that he seemed pleased by the fact that he could beat up all these people. He grinned, still hitting the Bobo. After this he found the gun again and started shooting at the Bobo, pretending the Bobo was the bad guy. This play began to have a somewhat more organized character as he hid behind a beanbag to shoot at the Bobo. Again, he did not involve me in the game or want me to become part of it.

At this point I began a running commentary on his play; one comment was that he was fighting with the bad guy. He said, "Yeah, I got to kill the bad guys." I wondered out loud who the special bad guys in his life were. He looked in my direction for a second and then grabbed the ball and started throwing it in my direction. I wondered out loud if he thought I was a bad guy. He looked away and started throwing the ball more frantically. I commented that sometimes bad guys can be scary. He then switched back to the racing cars and, still moving at a fairly frantic pace, began looking in my direction more frequently. He did not on his own, however, allow for any interactive game or communication with me.

The end of the interview was approaching, and I suggested that he might enjoy doing some drawing. He immediately took the crayons, pen, and pencil and started throwing them at the Bobo as though they were knives. In response to my firmly structured suggestion, he agreed to sit down and draw something. First, he showed me how he makes letters at school. As indicated above, I noticed that his capacity to form letters was less than optimal for his age. When I suggested he draw a picture of his family, he rebelled against the idea and instead said that he was going to draw a forest, which became multicolored, disorganized circles. In response to questions about his family, he said that his mother was a good cook. With regard to his father, he said, "He hits me." He responded with silence when I asked him about his brother. When I asked whether he ever had any dreams, he shook his head to mean no. He may not have understood what I meant by dreams, even though I explained about seeing pictures when he closes his eyes. He ended the interview without any particular emotional reaction but was able to shake hands in response to my reaching out my hand.

## COMMENTS

Harold was a healthy, good-sized 7½-year-old. In terms of physical and neurological status, his gross motor coordination seemed quite appropriate. However, his fine motor coordination, as indicated by his inability to form certain letters, seemed below the age-appropriate level and raised some questions about his perceptual motor capacity. Moreover, he seemed to lack a capacity for focused concentration, as evidenced by his being in constant motion in both the waiting room and the playroom. With some effort on my part he could become focused, but was always easily distracted. Further, the capacity for developing organized themes, which he showed to some extent, was interfered with by his need to be in constant motion. He seemed reasonably intelligent in the way that he dealt with the playroom and developed his games. Although there was no special opportunity for seeing what his level of intelligence was, it did not appear to be outside age-appropriate norms.

Harold made human contact with me only through glances. Although the number of glances increased slightly toward the end of the interview, there was no deepening sense of relatedness. He made almost no attempt to involve me in his play or to communicate directly with me. It was as though I was just another object in the room of which he took note and was cautious. The only affective relatedness to me was around the theme of "the bad guys." It is possible that his constant activity may have been working against a more latent capacity for developing relatedness. With a child his age one would expect a deepening warmth and sense of relatedness in the context of a variety of affects and themes. With this child, however, the capacity for relatedness was not at the expected level.

His mood was stable throughout and could be described as one of wild excitement combined with some apprehension. The way he constantly moved around certainly had an excited quality to it; yet there was also the sense of apprehension, particularly when he was involved in the shooting game with the bad guys.

The main affects he showed were his concerns with competition, winning, and being powerful, along with some indication of fear. There was little expression of warmth, empathy, love, or real curiosity about what was available to him in the room, or available from communicating with me. When I wondered whether I was the bad guy, his anxiety was reflected in the way he quickly shifted activities and increased the activity level. This shift did not show a severe disruption; rather, it was a quickening of the pace of his already heightened activity level. He showed an ability to continue evolving the themes, however. Overall, particularly in terms of his range and types of affects, he seemed to be struggling with affective concerns slightly below the 7½-year-old level, more like a 5-year-old level where concern about power, competition, winning, losing, and fear of bad guys would be expected to dominate.

In spite of the immoderately high level of activity, Harold was able to show a capacity for small units of organized themes which hung together when reviewed in the perspective of the entire interview. That is, the themes of winning, aggression, competition, power, and eventually good guys and bad guys were presented in an organized fashion. It was notable, however, that these themes were presented in fragments or, one could say, that his dramas were divided into short and disconnected acts of very intense activity, in contrast both to acts that have continuity with each other and to acts that are longer, more leisurely, and thus more fully developed. Here again, it seemed that his activity level interfered with his ability to focus his concentration. There was some development of themes, but not the rich, deepening development that might be expected from a 7½-year-old. Harold kept the themes of power, competition, aggression, winning and losing, and good and bad guys at a fairly concrete, superficial level, revealing little about what was behind these concerns.

The sequence of his themes progressed from racing, winning and losing, and being Superman, to fighting with bad guys and protecting himself from the bad forces. The sequence reveals a series of concerns more at the 5- or 5½-year-old level, as indicated above; that is, concerns with power, aggression, size, and opposing forces trying to overwhelm him.

My initial subjective reactions concerned being hit by the ball that he was throwing somewhat wildly. After the initial danger seemed over, I hoped to develop a deeper and richer communication. When such communication did not occur, however, I felt disappointed that an empathic rapport could not be established with this child. I did feel some relief that he was able to respond to structure during the interview and that the chaotic and frenzied activity did not intensify but, rather, slowed down as he got to know me better.

## Case 3

*Interview*

As I entered the waiting room Joan, almost 6, was standing. She looked rather shy and did not speak. I suggested that she come into the playroom and she did. She was cute, well-built, and apparently well-coordinated in both her gross and fine motor actions. She walked in a firm, confident manner and later showed she was able to draw and do other fine motor activities successfully.

She came into the room cautiously, walking slowly at first and not saying anything. She went to the Bobo first, grabbed his red nose, and said that it was not supposed to stick out. There was a slightly nasal, lispy quality to her speech which diminished as the session went on. She seemed almost too relaxed and passive. She took no initiative to open a dialogue, nor did she explore much of the room. After a few minutes I broke the stillness by saying that she was free to play with anything or talk about anything she wished. I told her the rules of the playroom: we could not hurt each other or break anything. She immediately went over to the desk and began drawing.

She drew a picture of a little girl. What looked like a beard was, she told me, jewelry the girl was wearing. She then spontaneously told me that she was born here in Washington, and that her little sister thought that she was born here, too, but she was actually born in Long Island. Upon inquiry she told me that she meant her 4-year-old sister. She then started talking about her brother as though I knew all about him. As she elaborated I discovered that he was 8 years old and that he used to be in a special math class. She talked about math and science repetitiously, using the same few ideas again and again. Then she told me that she knew her teacher's first name, and smiled as though she knew something she was not supposed to know. She revealed that she did not like Sunday school and did not like to go because of having to leave her dog, Winnie. She made a joke about Winnie-the-Pooh and laughed. She seemed to be relaxed and enjoying herself at this time, about midway through the session.

She told me that she had a best friend. Joan was finishing a drawing of a big girl in a small house, the house just fitting around the girl. There was also a small car. I asked her to tell me more about the girl, but she told me about the house instead. She said that something was wrong with the chimney: the chimney was pink, and pink things can fall off. She appeared relaxed. I asked if she could tell me more about the girl and the chimney and the roof. She replied that the girl was Little Red Ridinghood and then she drew a picture of the wolf pretending to be grandmother.

At this point, immediately after she talked about the wolf pretending to be grandmother, she started inquiring about the mirrors on the wall (they were one-way observation windows) with some curiosity and suspiciousness. Although she had not shown a great deal of exploration on a motor level, staying mostly in one spot, she now acted curious and started walking around the room and looking at things. I commented that Little Red Ridinghood must have been scared and unsure about the wolf, must have felt uncertain seeing as how her grandmother could be a wolf. I continued, "Maybe Joan feels a little uncertain with all these mirrors in the room, being in a strange place, not knowing what's going to happen, just like Red Ridinghood."

She was silent after my comment. She tore off the sheet of paper that she was drawing on and seemed to become decidedly apprehensive in her own quiet way. She then went over to the blackboard and asked me for some chalk. I told her that there was no chalk in the room and asked what she wanted to write. She said something about writing "yes" and "you." She was not clear, and I could only wonder whether the "yes" was to signify that I was right, that she was feeling uneasy.

The chalk being unavailable to her, I offered some alternatives. She seemed more suspicious and apprehensive, but even with this anxiety, she began to communicate more with me. She looked out the window, then noticed a policeman doll in the playroom. She took the doll and flirted with the idea of dropping it out the window. She became coy with me and wanted to know if it was all right to drop the doll. She then said that I had taken all this from her, referring to the play materials on the desk. She said, "These are all mine. I'm taking them home with me."

She started to play with the toilet, which was part of the dollhouse, and began sticking all the dolls into the toilet. She put one doll on the toilet and then put its head in the toilet. I made a comment about the doll going into the toilet headfirst. She put another girl doll on top of the doll on the toilet, and then tried to stick everyone in together. She seemed to become more relaxed as she was doing this, and she giggled. Then she tried to take the baby doll's diaper off. This was hard for her to do because the diaper was made of cellophane. She wanted me to close my eyes as she hid the baby doll. Then I was to guess where it was. (At a number of points throughout the interview she had wanted me to guess what she was drawing, thinking, saying, or doing.) She then went over to the blocks and began building an incline. She showed me how it worked, and began talking about a science project at school.

As the end of the interview was near, I asked if she ever had any dreams (a question I frequently ask in such sessions). Openly and without hesitation, she told me the following dream. She said, "Me, Pam, and Michael were walking home from school and there were these witches. It was Halloween before we got home, and then we were eating dinner and the witches gave us this bread, which had poison, and father ate the bread and fell off his chair. And then it was morning and I woke up." I said, "That sounds like a scary dream." Without comment she took a block and put it under her dress near her vagina. Immediately afterward, again showing curiosity, she came over to me and asked what I was doing. She pointed at my notes and asked what I was writing there. With a knowing look she indicated to me that my writing made her uneasy, that she did not want anything down on paper.

She then told me about a 2-year-old boy who said that water did not scare him any more. She went on to tell me about her interest in baking a cake, and then told me that once her mother had stolen Hanukkah money from her and her sister. She was able to acknowledge that she got mad at her mother, and she said that she never got the money back. Apparently her mother had confessed to her that she had in fact taken Joan's money because she was short of shopping money. The session closed at this point.

COMMENTS

It was clear that Joan's motor coordination was appropriately intact for a 6-year-old.

Her emotional tone, although basically one of shyness, embraced the capacity to evolve a relationship with the interviewer. In terms of relations, she demonstrated an appropriate capacity for attachment. The initial shyness evolved into openness with and relatedness to the interviewer. This relatedness was differentiated around the thematic material. That is, she was able to integrate a sense of interpersonal relatedness with the themes that she was developing. It was not clear whether her level of interpersonal relatedness was predominantly dyadic or triangular.

In terms of the style and development of affect, Joan was quietly cautious, seductive, guarded, suspicious, and apprehensive. There were mild signs of aggression in her coyness and teasing, and a blatant display of hostility when she stuffed all the dolls into the toilet. There was little expression of empathy, warmth, or love, which raises some question about her capacity for, or access to, these affects. She made the quick shifts characteristic of anxiety by showing apprehension and then curiosity (asking questions first about the mirrors and then about my notes). Although she experienced definite points of anxiety during the interview, it is important to note that this anxiety was not disorganizing, nor did it disrupt the interpersonal relatedness or the sequence of themes that were evolving. Interestingly, the first abrupt shift to curiosity (leading to questions about the mirrors) followed the themes of either houses or little girls being too big or small, chimneys, things falling off, and whether or not grandmother (the interviewer?) was a wolf in disguise. This sequence suggests anxiety about size, attachments falling off and people tricking one another.

With regard to Joan's use of the space, she was quite passive and shy at first. Later on, however, she was able to expand and use the room and its objects to tell her story. Following the rules, she did not break or throw things. Nevertheless, she teased me with the policeman doll: "I'm going to throw him out. Will you let me?" This shows that she can readily internalize structure and is able to regulate herself reasonably well.

Turning to the category of thematic development, Joan showed an age-appropriate capacity to organize thematic material in a continuous and relevant way; that is, her themes were logically connected from the beginning to the end of the interview. She was somewhat repetitious both in her themes of destruction, anger, and things falling off, and in her displays of coquettishness and seductiveness. The developmental level of these themes was not made clear.

There was a certain depth and richness to the material she presented in terms of her ability to be in touch with her feelings. Although there may have been some walling off of feelings in the positive realm, she was in touch with a wide range of negative feelings. Expressing them made her somewhat anxious, but this anxiety did not overwhelm her.

Some question remains about the age-appropriateness of the thematic material. Were her themes more appropriate for a younger child? There was little indication of repression during the session, and we do not know whether she has in fact reached the developmental point of intense triangular concerns. She might still be involved with her own bodily integrity and concerns—particularly around aggression. We want to keep in mind such questions about age-appropriateness when taking a history from parents. We will also use psychological testing and possibly more playroom interviews to help answer these questions.

The final comment takes note of my subjective experience of Joan. Throughout the interview I was aware of a conflict between wishing to provide more structure and watching to see what she would develop on her own. I did not feel any warmth of involvement with her although she was clearly attempting to relate to me in a reasonably warm and somewhat open manner.

**Case 4**

*Interview*

When I first saw Cathy she was standing, looking somewhat sad and frightened, and holding onto her mother in a shy, fearful manner. She did not look at me. Later, when it was her time to come into the interview room, she was in another playroom assiduously washing utensils. A female assistant was there with her. When I entered this scene, again she did not look at me although she knew it was time to come into the other room with me. I said to her, "We'll go into the other room," and she finished cleaning up and came with me easily enough. Cathy was nearly 6 years old and had excellent motor control over both gross and fine movements. As I noted later, her speech was very clear and she was unusually verbal.

After coming into the playroom with me, her affective tone changed remarkably. She smiled broadly in a flirtatious way. She gave the Bobo a big punch with a joyous, playful expression. She wanted to know why it did not get back up. Then she explored the rest of the room in a rather calm and relaxed style, picking up and examining things. Then she quickly went over and set up the doll family and the chairs and table. Looking at the toilet, she said, "I can use this as a chair . . . no, I've got to clean it." When I inquired about this, she said, "Well, there are germs and I've got to clean it." She did not, however, make any attempt to go to the room where she had been washing utensils.

She asked if her brother (whom I had also seen) had come in here, and then immediately went to punch the Bobo. I inquired if she liked to punch her brother, and she answered that it was exciting to fight. Then she said, "Okay, Bobo, you've had it." She said that the Bobo came up behind her and shoved her. She then began kicking and biting the Bobo and pushing its head back, describing her actions to me. She expressed some concern that the air might go out of it. When I commented that it seemed she did not want to hurt the Bobo too much, she agreed that was the case. Next she went to the rocking horse and said, "It's too little for me," indicating that she was not a baby anymore.

She then went around the room and asked if she had lots of time to play. I could not tell whether she wanted time to play or, on the contrary, wanted to leave soon. I was inclined to the latter interpretation, however, because of her very ambiguity. My impression at this time was that her saying, "No, no, I want to play as long as I can because I'm having a good time," was the opposite of what she was feeling.

She began printing letters; she spelled S-O-X, then said, "I goofed," and scribbled all over the letters. This behavior seemed to represent some degree of organization and freedom, and yet disorganization at the same time. She asked if she could draw on the table. When I asked what she thought about that, she gave up. She then said, "My mother doesn't let me scribble on the table at home. We don't have much at home." I inquired about this and she said that her father brought paper to her, perhaps indicating that "daddy" was, in her view, the giving, nurturing figure.

She then discovered a salt container and began putting salt on the paper. She put some on her clothing and said, "This is my uniform at school. See how clean it is." Then, under the guise of making the paper clean, she began spilling salt all over it. Pouring out salt, she became very excited as it spilled all over the paper and the toy animals. I commented on her excitement and she said that her mother did not allow her to do that. She quickly went back to the salt, saying, "I think I'll eat some," and she tried to give some to the baby dolls. She put salt in a baby bottle and indicated that the dolls did not like it. She tried it herself and said, "I don't like it." She was also concerned about getting the salt in a small cut she had on her hand. Then she gave some salt to the toy hippo and pretended that he liked it.

She said she needed a spoon and wanted to go to the other playroom to get one. Since the door to the other room was locked, I suggested that we find something else she could use. She found a small dump truck for the purpose, easily adjusting to the fact that she could not have a spoon. She put salt on the crayons and was delighted with messing with the salt. She put salt on the rug, and I told her she should not because that made it difficult for the people cleaning the room. She tested the limits by first putting a little more salt on the rug and then putting some on the table.

I commented about the difference between here and home, that maybe she was concerned about the things that she could or could not do. I asked how she felt about the freedom she was experiencing here. She told me, "I throw things at home. I threw something at my mother." She then quickly said, "No, I didn't. I'm just making up a story." A moment later she said, "I kick Mother." Then added, "No, I don't. I'm just making up a story." I asked, "Would you like to kick Mother?" She said, "Yes, but I don't want to hurt her feelings." She then went back to the salt, pretending it was water, and began pouring it on the mother doll. She said the mother and a little girl were drowning in the water. Then she pulled them out, saying that they had jumped out. Next she put them in the washer and washed their hands.

She inquired about the time, and I asked how much more time she wanted. She said she wanted lots of time to play, which I again thought was an ambivalent response.

She said, "I hope Mark [her brother] stays out there" (in the waiting room). I asked if she was feeling at all anxious. She indicated that she was not, but she wanted to know if she and her mother were on time. She said she thought that they were late. She then indicated that she wanted to go into the other room where there were more toys and a sink.

At this point she went to the phone, which seemed to express a need to make an attachment either to Mark or her mother. I suggested that we could have a make-believe telephone conversation and talk to anyone she wished. She said, "You be John." She told me that John was her older brother who was in the Navy; he was stationed in a place where they make bombs and missiles. After telling me he was 18, she asked, "Is that too young to be a soldier?" Another question followed quickly: "How old are you?" Her affect was very flirtatious at this time and she came very close to me. Her closeness made me slightly anxious. I commented that she was curious about me and that maybe she could tell a story about me or about any thoughts that she had. She said, "You're a soldier and you make bombs. Let's pretend you're 18." I asked "You mean, like your brother?" She then quickly went over and began hitting the Bobo. She said, "He makes me mad." I made a comment about her missing her brother since there seemed to be some relation between that possibility and punching the Bobo.

She asked if what she was telling me was going to be private. When I inquired about this, she said she would not want her mother to know. I asked what in particular she did not want her mother to know. She said, "Mother once threw a hamburger at Daddy. No, that's a story." Then, when I inquired, she said, "Yes, but it missed Daddy." I asked her about her father and she said, "Daddy has black hair. He's kind of dopey. He punches everyone once in a while." Then, "Oh, that's a story, too."

At the end of the interview I did some structuring by asking if anything scared her. She answered with slight excitement, "The doctor . . . giant monster . . . he goes 'ahh.' " She began jumping about, pretending to be a monster. I commented that maybe sometimes she liked to be the monster.

She said yes, and indicated that she had terrible dreams of monsters; but again, the affect was one of joyous expansiveness. Then, telling me she was the monster, she came and punched me in the arm. She told me that she liked to make up stories, monster stories in particular. She began looking in some drawers and became very curious. The hour was up and I said that we would have to stop. She said she had more stories and I asked her to tell me the best one. The story again dealt with a monster and aggression. Her behavior near the end of the interview was both curious and seductive. Her looking in the drawers had the flavor of snooping—she pretended that no one knew what she was doing. She ended the session with a "good-bye" to me and a smile indicating some pleasure.

### COMMENTS

Cathy appeared to be physically intact and extraordinarily bright for her age. While she was able to regress freely and develop rich fantasies when given permission, she could also progress and respond to structure when it was indicated. Her verbal ability was unusually good.

Her overall emotional tone was one of joy and curiosity. She related in an intensely personal and intimate manner, constantly yet pleasantly insisting on my attention with her chatting and questions. Her relatedness showed a controlling quality as well as a seductive intrusiveness.

She demonstrated mostly joyous, explorative, excited affects of a wide age-appropriate range and depth during the course of the interview. As indicated, there was some show of diffuse anger, but in a playful way (with the Bobo doll), so that the anger seemed to be neutralized. Because of the expressive content of her anger—and yet little real display of anger—one may wonder about her tolerance for this affect. She showed some anxiety but was quite able to make transitions and continue her themes. Optimally, one might have expected a little more fearfulness and more negative affects; however, I gather from her references to her mother that she may show such feelings more with women than with men. Toward the end of the session, she became very flirtatious.

She took little time to begin exploring the entire playroom. Her play themes developed throughout the session and revealed a rich fantasy life that she had some control over. She revealed some conflicts, which she was able to deal with in a flexible way. She showed concern about doing well when she scribbled on a piece of paper, and wanted to know if she had goofed. She also seemed concerned about how organized or disorganized

82

she was permitted to be, and looked for direct feedback from me. However, these hesitations were minor asides to her basically explorative, open, and fun-loving affective manner.

Although Cathy's opening themes spoke of some conflict with messing and cleaning, she seemed to use the occasion of mother's absence to throw caution to the wind. It is possible that she feels freer with men than with women. She indicated feelings of both anger and fright toward her mother. Her feelings toward her father, who she said was sort of dopey, were not clear. She revealed complicated feelings about her brother, showing some difficulty with her aggressive and fearful feelings related to his absence—she quickly shifted gears when discussions of her brother emerged.

In the beginning I felt quite relaxed with Cathy. Her demand for engagement by continuously looking at me and directing questions to me diminished as the interview went on, although I was always aware of her need to control. At one time I felt the conflict between how much I was to control the session and how much she was to control it. In the latter part of the interview, when she asked how old I was, I began feeling uneasy. The anxious feeling also occurred when she asked how much time we had, because I felt that she wanted to leave. In general, she was able to arouse in me a variety of feelings around such issues as control, intrusiveness, and abandonment. I was impressed with both the variety and the continuity of her affects throughout the session. As the above comments suggest, her overall functioning seemed to be age-appropriate.

### Case 5

*Interview*

When I entered the waiting room to greet Steve, a 6½-year-old boy, he was crawling under the couch, making high-pitched gleeful sounds. His mother looked worried. All the magazines were strewn over the floor. He came along easily, if not a bit overenthusiastically, into my office. He tripped over his own feet, walking with a wide, somewhat unstable gait. His words were indistinct as he talked in a slightly hoarse voice, ran words together quickly, and mispronounced many sounds. Yet he was understandable. His fine motor coordination was quite clumsy as he quickly went searching through the toy closet, dropping small items and having difficulty manipulating the smaller, finer toys. Later he had difficulty in drawing circles and squares, etc.

He made fleeting, mildly impersonal contact with me through a quick glance and immediately thereafter went to the toys. A frantic quality quickly emerged as he tossed all the toys on the floor in a disorganized manner. He then kept asking me to name each toy and other objects in the room. When I commented on his "interest in knowing names of things," he again made fleeting eye contact and kept asking me to name items.

He kept moving, at times running, around the room, looking excited, occasionally tripping, momentarily looking confused, and then would become excited again.

This pattern went on for about 10 minutes. He then came across a stick and, with a gleeful look, repetitively banged it against a chair. He then jumped on some crayons that I had spilled on the floor, and, taking a policeman doll, he began banging it on the floor, saying "Bad boy, bad boy." He momentarily looked "blank" and began rocking back and forth while sitting on the floor.

He then looked at me and asked, "Do you have any candy?" I commented that he wanted me to give him some candy, and he said "yes" and then started to throw a sponge ball at me, not stopping until I physically restrained him. He then said, "I want that horse" (a rubber play horse).

Nearing the end of the interview, I asked him about his parents, school, dreams, etc., and he only answered with regard to school, talking about "hitting kids" and "being bad." He named some children, but would not elaborate.

He left the interview still quite active, with a fleeting glance.

COMMENTS

Physical and neurological development appeared significantly below age expectations, as evidenced by his difficulties with gross and fine motor coordination, hoarse and indistinct speech, difficulty with modulating his activity level and impulses. There was also a perseverative quality to his questions—"What's this?" etc.—and a ritualistic quality to some activities such as banging. In addition, there was a brief episode of rocking. All these observations raise questions about physical-neurological compromises.

Mood vacillated between undifferentiated excitement and an indifferent quality. He related to me but only fleetingly, with little depth. Relatedness was therefore also below age expectations. There was little of the age-appropriate range of affects or modulation (e.g., only undifferentiated excitement). Anxiety may be inferred in relation to the loss of relatedness (i.e., blank look), rocking, and the impulsiveness (e.g., throwing a ball at me) that occurred after the "bad boy" theme and request for candy.

The interview suggested that anxiety is disruptive to an already vulnerable neurophysiological integrative capacity and may be experienced at the most primitive level of somatic disorganization.

Thematic concerns were communicated in the following sequence: aggressiveness, loss of control, being a "bad boy," disorganization, hunger, anger. They reflected islands of cohesive thematic interests. Organization, range, and depth were all significantly below age expectations. By age 6½ cohesive, rich themes would be expected. There were no highly "bizarre" themes, however.

Subjective reactions vacillated between apprehension about his impulsiveness, lack of involvement, and some relief at the fleeting eye contact, indicating a potential for involvement.

## Case 6

*Interview*

David entered the interview room with a relaxed though somewhat clumsy gait. He was talking freely in a friendly way and his facial expression was relaxed. As the session progressed, he showed good gross and fine motor coordination and good modulation of his activity level. His contact with me was warm and friendly. He took in the entire room and was quite curious and exploratory in a reasonably systematic yet spontaneous and relaxed way. In short, in terms of his initial orientation to me and the room, he behaved quite up to the optimal expectations for his age of 5½ years.

He went to the racing cars first and told me that a tire was broken. Then he went around to all the toys, picking up and examining each one. He put on a cowboy hat, which fell off. He then began playing with the dolls and identified a father, mother, and son doll on his own. He said, "Hey, these things are puppets," and began playing with them. He talked about the mother doll sending some of the puppets to another part of the room. He went over to the gun and told me that it was broken (because he could not work it). He then told me that the cars did not run well, but played with them for a while. He developed a slight theme with the cars and got them going all over the place.

All this time David was friendly, but then, in the context of the car game, he showed me that he knew karate. He informed me that the son (doll) was having to take care of the daddy (doll) because the daddy's car had broken down. When I asked him whether the son had a better car, he got the son and father puppets and developed an elaborate story about the son's wanting to karate chop the father because the son could not get enough Coke to drink. The son and father got into a fight with the son trying to kill the father. Then the father gave the son a lecture, after which the son beat up the mother, saying, "I want a Coke." Finally the son got hurt and the mother kissed him and said, "You were a bad boy." The story ended with the son lying face down.

This story lasted for about 15 minutes and was related very expressively, with David doing the talking for all parties. I was watchful but not particularly supportive, occasionally commenting in order to follow up on themes.

Soon after David finished this elaborate Oedipal theme with the son beating up the father in the mother's presence, he wanted to go back to the other room. My own associations at this point were that, having had his catharsis, he now wanted to get away from the scene of the action. I asked about his wish to leave and told him he could return to the other room later. He then quickly picked up some animals and wanted to know what I was writing. He picked up another animal and said that it was a mother rabbit, a theme he stayed with for a while without actually developing it. I inquired about the anger he had shown in the earlier scene and wondered about what happens when he gets angry. He told me that when he gets angry he throws things and karate chops his brother. He said this happens when he does not get to go outside. He then went back to the dolls, further developing the theme of aggression. He then talked about the dolls liking each other, but he placed them face down.

We were now near the end of the session. I asked about mother and he said, "Very nice." He picked up a car and then an animal, and said about the latter, "This is a dinosaur." I asked him about father and he said, "I don't know. I don't know anything about him, but I know he is very nice —he is a lawyer." Then he came back to his mother, saying, "Don't know about Mommy." Then he started talking about a little girl named Mary Lou who was very nice. He then commented that there were not as many toys here as in the other room and started telling me about a friend called Robbie "who is a mean person who throws things." I asked about his sister; he said that she was nice and that his brother was very nice. I asked if he had any dreams, and he told me he had a dream about Winnie-the-Pooh doing something naughty and awakening the Scottie puppy. He ended the interview in a relaxed fashion without any particular affective expression.

COMMENTS

David appeared to be a physically intact child with reasonably clear speech. He was personable in manner, maintaining good contact throughout the interview. He demonstrated an overall quality of curiosity and warmth, and showed capacities for pleasure and enjoyment as well. He related to the interviewer with interest but without any deepening of affect. He did not ask questions but developed one particularly rich theme and a few subthemes largely on his own.

He demonstrated a rich variety of age-appropriate emotions but his main concerns were with anger, competition, and with not getting enough feeding. When he got anxious and wanted to leave after the family drama was elaborated, he was quickly able to shift his attention to other things when told there was more time remaining.

He was both explorative and organized in the playroom. He dealt with themes of anger by displacing them into games, yet showed that he understood the limits of the playroom.

During the interview, David developed a cohesive and organized theme focusing on the family struggle and fighting with father. Most impressive was the way he played the theme out by modulating the emotions and affects of each party. The theme of family aggression and conflict dominated the session; no equally rich thematic development occurred around his pleasurable pursuits except in reference to wanting a Coke from his parents.

Subjectively, interaction with David generated interest in the interviewer but did not induce any feelings of personal intimacy. The interviewer felt intellectually but not emotionally enriched by the experience, suggesting that perhaps this child tends to limit the depth of affect he permits himself in his family dramas.

As suggested above, David's functioning is in the age-appropriate range.

### Case 7

*Interview*

Joey was a trifle small for his age of 5¼ years, and his voice was slightly nasal or lispy. He was sucking his thumb and holding onto his mother when

I first met him. He announced, "I won't let her go," and said to her, "I'm going with you." His mother cajoled him, attempted to bribe and manipulate him in various ways, but could not get him to go into the playroom without her.

Although apprehensive, he moved slowly and evenly, and appeared to have good gross and fine motor coordination. He avoided eye contact with me, looking instead at his mother as if to deny my presence. Anxious though he seemed, there was a grin on his face when engaged in the verbal battle with mother about whether she would stay in the playroom with him. He did explore the playroom to an extent, but stayed close to mother. She seemed reluctant to give him directions.

As the session went on he relaxed somewhat, talking with me and glancing at me from time to time. Throughout, however, the basic and major tie was to mother. It was difficult to assess the degree to which he was indeed frightened and the degree to which he was receiving gratification from manipulating his mother. Interestingly, the mother tried in numerous ways to get him to stay on his own, including telling him later in the interview that she "had to go to the bathroom or I'll make in my pants." To this he responded that he would accompany her and stand outside the bathroom.

Once in the playroom with mother, he sat on the Bobo and pulled its nose, announcing, "I'm going to let the air out." He looked at me to see if I was angry and then proceeded to let the air out. After playing with the Bobo he said he wanted to draw. He drew and tried to write his name. He then moved on to lining up some play animals and announced to me that the giraffe was the biggest one. He then became concerned about the window being open and wanted to close it. I asked him about that and his response was to threaten to throw one of the animals out of the window. Overall, his manner was characterized by a mildly provocative, controlling quality with brief shifts to coy pleasure and occasional displays of apprehension.

He went to the toy dog and announced that it was the smallest animal. I asked how he thought the dog felt being the smallest and, after some deliberation, he said, "They will eat him up." When I said, "That must be pretty scary," he went over and began bouncing the ball. He proceeded to pick up a horse and then figures of a cowboy and an Indian. He found a gun which he pointed at his mother, and then became angry, saying, "Why doesn't it work? Where's the bullet? It's lost." He then became involved with the fireman and the cowboy and tried on their hats. He announced that the hats were both too small, and then said that one was too big and one was too small. He then wanted to know if there was a television set in the room. I said there was none and asked about his interest in TV. He discussed with me the possibility of his putting on a TV show. Then he picked up the man puppet and, putting it near his mother's face, said, "He is crying." Shortly after that he went out of the room with mother, accompanying her to the bathroom as referred to above.

By the time they returned, the interview was almost over, and I began to structure the final moments. I asked, "If you could have three wishes, what would they be?" He said for the first wish, he would want nothing; for the second wish, he said, "I want a real gun with real bullets to shoot people—only bad people, but people who fight with me." I inquired about people who fight with him and he told me about his friend Jimmy: "He beats me up." For the third wish, he first wanted a basketball and then decided on a Bobo doll because he liked hitting the Bobo.

Interestingly, it was during this phase of the interview, when I was asking specific questions, that I felt he was more relaxed with me. I asked if he ever had dreams. It was unclear whether what he proceeded to tell me were real dreams, pieces of TV shows that he had watched, or daydreams. Nevertheless, he reported something about TV shows and a witch and two small children who sneak up on the witch's house. There was someone in the house with a long mustache and a beard. He did not go on. I proceeded by asking about any scary dreams, and he told me, "We all saw a movie and my brother threw up in the toilet. My brother had to sleep with Mommy in the same room." He also told how he had bad dreams after watching the movie and was scared that he was going to be locked in somewhere. During this recital he kept looking at his mother. I then asked if he had any questions for me. He proceeded to bring me a dead insect that he had found and told me a little dog had scared the insect. He then stood up next to his mother, took the gun out, and said, "Is time up?" I said that it was and ended our session.

COMMENTS

Although small for his age, Joey seemed to be neurologically sound, with his gross and fine motor coordination and perceptual motor ability all apparently intact. His overall mood was one of apprehension. Predominant affects demonstrated in the interview were the tendency to cling, apprehension, and anger—although there was a facade of playful and pleasurable manipulativeness around the issue of control. He needed to keep mother with him. The anxiety he manifested seemed to center on separation and aggression. When he related to me, the quality was mostly one of apprehension. As indicated, he responded better when I structured things for him with questions, which enabled him to relate to me somewhat warmly. Even then, however, there was only minimal affective depth and his tone was one of reluctance. For the most part, his was a superficial yet distinctly human involvement with the interviewer. Control, provocativeness (teasing), and the use of distance characterized his style of relatedness.

He did not deal with the entire playroom but tended to stay in one area, usually near mother. Nor did he develop cohesive themes, but rather, moved from one thing to another. These bits and pieces had little richness. In a limited way he was able to dramatize some of his conflicts around the issues of aggression, his tie to mother, his feeling small, and his experience of danger. He showed some concerns about being engulfed orally (e.g., the little dog being eaten up) and about castration (e.g., shooting). He demonstrated a dependency on mother which seemed below his age-appropriate level. His mother seemed to be unable to help him resolve this attachment and in some respects played into his hands.

My initial subjective feeling was one of discomfort at his unwillingness to separate from mother. However, I soon found myself calmly enjoying the scene of mother's struggles with him, feeling relieved that I was not in her place. Even though he became more related to me, I did not feel involved with or interested in him. I was not in touch with any fantasies during the session which, on the whole, I found neither difficult nor pleasurable.

As this summary suggests, Joey was functioning below age expectations for a 5¼-year-old in almost all the descriptive areas.

## Case 8

*Interview*

For a few moments, I was able to observe Mark in the waiting room with his parents. He was a blond-haired 4½-year-old, extremely tall, strongly and thickly built. He walked with an unusual gait, stepping first onto his toes, then flopping down to his heels, while his arms moved every which way in a purposeless but not quite spastic fashion. I saw him toss a ball to his father and follow instructions from his parents. When I offered my hand to him and asked him to come into the office, he refused and moved away from me in his special, uncoordinated style, running to his mother's lap. After a few moments of patient, expectant waiting, I suggested that the family come in together.

In the playroom Mark seemed able to understand and carry out even complex instructions from his parents, which they eagerly volunteered. ("Show Dr. Greenspan how you play.") The child quickly made eye contact with me and even started to move in my direction, but then made a fast retreat and jumped in mother's lap. His father insisted that he get down and play, which he did. His quality of relatedness to me, and even somewhat to his parents, was unusual in that he would make fleeting contact and then seemingly lose contact, his eyes taking on a glazed, preoccupied appearance. Unlike a youngster who makes contact and then becomes negative and breaks it off, Mark would make a quick contact and then seem to become confused or disorganized. After such contact he would shift in another direction and often behave aimlessly for a few moments.

During the early part of the interview, while his parents were encouraging him to play, he would say things—e.g., "The wolf is coming"—from out of the blue. For example, when he commented that the wolf was coming, he was not playing with the toy wolf, nor had there been any prior mention of animals or of people being attacked. On occasion throughout the interview he would start to approach me, then change this action to running to mother or father and wanting to be held. At times, he would aggressively pinch mother or father, and they would become angry and slap him, insisting that he "go back on the floor and show Dr. Greenspan how you play."

In about the middle of the interview Mark got angry, seemingly without provocation, and started screaming, "I want to go." This outburst rapidly took on the quality of a tantrum as he stamped up and down and jumped about with his floppy leg movements and uncoordinated arm movements. His voice had a slightly gruff quality but was clear and distinct. His statement, "I want to go," was the most purposeful one he made during the entire interview. When his parents did not respond to this demand, he went over and pinched one of them. Then he proceeded to wander around the room for a few minutes in a seemingly confused state. He did not approach any of the toys or other play materials; he did not develop any activity.

After he had explored a little of the room in this random way, he went to mother and somewhat gently sat in her lap and cuddled in her arms. Within a moment of seeming to be warm to her, he said, "I hurt you if we don't go." Mother responded supportively, again directing him to the toys on the floor. He was then able to begin building a tower of blocks. This was by far his most organized performance during the session. While their son was thus engaged in focused concentration, father appeared to be uncomfortable and mother seemed to show sympathy and warmth. At one point the father insisted, "Get me a duck from over there." This command had the effect of distracting Mark's focus on building the tower.

As the interview progressed, mother looked increasingly depressed and withdrawn; she did not seem to know how to "get Mark to perform better." Father grew increasingly impatient and his sporadic outbursts of "do this" and "do that" became angry demands. Meanwhile, Mark continued to explore the toys in his random way. He touched things and occasionally put little dolls or blocks in his mouth. At one point his mother asked him what color something was and he was able to say it was orange; then his father asked him to spell it and he spelled it correctly.

At times Mark would refuse to get down from his mother's lap by saying, "I want to sit on your lap." Once when he was sitting there, he put a pencil in his mouth and began holding his genitals. Sometimes when he walked around, he would begin almost shaking with excitement, stretching out his arms in every direction and moving his fingers and arms up and down randomly. He occasionally said words that were incomprehensible, seemingly tying together syllables from different words. He also uttered sentences from out of the blue, such as, "I have poison in my mouth." At one point, when his parents did not do what he asked, he threatened to stab them with a pencil and excitedly went at them until his father grabbed him. Throughout most of the interview his affects were bland and flat, although he showed chaotic excitement or confused bewilderment from time to time, as well as exhibiting an occasional interest in being held.

Near the end of the interview, still trying to demonstrate Mark's abilities, father asked him to name things, and he was able to identify many objects in the room. Father also got a book to show me how Mark could identify the pictures—which Mark did very well. Indeed, he demonstrated an overall ability to identify objects at or above his chronological age. Father also asked him to spell a few additional words, which he was able to do.

This pattern of showing occasional interest in the play material, wandering around the room, and jumping into mother's lap continued till the end of the interview, when Mark seemed happy to be able to leave with his parents. He showed little relatedness in saying good-bye; he looked away from me as he was leaving the office.

COMMENTS

This 4½-year-old boy showed some worrisome features in his overall physical and neurological development, that is, his unusual gait and uncoordinated arm movements. In many respects, his gait was reminiscent of a 14- or 15-month-old not yet comfortable with walking. He was able to formulate words reasonably well, however, and in play with some objects his fine motor coordination looked fairly good. His activity level was highly uneven —occasionally relaxed and focused, but often excited and very reactive. His overall mood seemed to be one of confusion and disorganization, with occasional breakthroughs of frustrated feelings and rage. His affect was mostly bland and flat except for occasional variations to an undifferentiated excited state or to a mild, partly frustrated, angry state. The absence of subtlety or range in his affect placed him well below age expectations in this category. His affective range was like that of a very anxious 1-year-old.

As described above, Mark made fleeting eye contact with me. He made more contact with his parents, especially with his mother; he behaved symbiotically in wanting to sit in her lap and be cuddled. His relatedness to me seemed disorganized—reminiscent of an 8- to 9-month-old having stranger anxiety. There was a worried look on his face when he glanced at me. For the most part, however, he did not relate to anyone other than mother—and then in a primitive symbiotic way—thus indicating that his capacity for relatedness was well below age expectations.

He seemed chronically anxious during the interview. The few themes that emerged concerned wolves, attacks, or poison. I speculated that his anxiety was related to fear of annihilation and bodily damage as well as to the more obvious concern about separation from mother. He was highly disorganized in his capacities to communicate with me and to develop any coherent themes. Most dramatic was the fragmented, piecemeal quality of his communications. On the whole, his behavior seemed random and chaotic, far below age expectations for a 4½-year-old. Indeed, such behavior would be considered below age expectations for a 15-month-old.

He was not able to develop themes with any richness or depth. The issues that emerged in the sequence of themes were wishing to be close to mother, feelings of violence when frustrated (e.g., "I'll stick a pencil in you"), and concerns about wolves attacking and being poisoned. There was general apprehension about exploring, interspersed with climbing into mother's lap for what appeared to be security and safety. Thus, the sequence of themes suggested concerns about separation and the most fundamental issues of security. In addition, a pronounced inability to deal with frustrated, angry impulses was evidenced by the overall disorganized quality of his communications.

My subjective reactions were concern for the explosive, violent quality that occasionally emerged, and exhaustion from watching the parents try to help their child become more organized. My initial impression was that this child was significantly below age expectations in most areas of functioning, including important areas such as relating to others and organizing communications. One exception was his well-developed capacity to name objects and spell, suggesting that the neurological basis of intellectual functioning may be at age level.

## Case 9

*First Interview*

Molly, a 4½-year-old, readily turned to me when I entered the waiting room. Showing a trace of eagerness on her otherwise expressionless face, she followed me into the office. She was well-built, slightly stocky, of average height, and walked in a clearly coordinated though somewhat "unfeminine" manner. Later in the interview she showed, through manipulation of crayons and drawing pencils, that her fine motor coordination was also quite well developed.

When she came into the room she gave me a rather straightforward yet cold look and asked in a slightly domineering tone, "Do you have a lollipop?" When I did not respond immediately, she explained, "I didn't get breakfast today. I threw up, I was sick." I commented that she must feel very hungry, and in return she gave me an expressionless look. Then she began to walk around and explore the room, occasionally turning toward me and commenting about what she saw, naming an ashtray and a book. Her vocabulary, her capacity for naming things, and her overall perceptiveness seemed quite well developed. As she talked and made eye contact with me, however, there was no expression of joy or pleasure. At times a sad, even depressed, quality came through.

After a brief exploration, she went to one corner of the room where she stood rather rigidly for the rest of the session. I went to where she was standing and apparently looking at a few objects on the table. She asked if I would be interested to "see how I can take off my shirt," adding quickly, "but I don't want to." Again there was a sad look; no flirtatious or joyous affect was associated with this comment. As a matter of fact, the discontinuity between her verbalization and her emotionless expression was striking.

After a few more minutes of looking around, she volunteered, "I like hard toys. I like stuffed animals." She then named a few things in the room and said, "I want to take these home." At one point she said she wanted to take the soap from the bathroom home. Such comments were often isolated and followed by silences. She did not say, for example, "Gee, there are many things here I would like to take home," and then list the items. A quality of affect hunger began to emerge and I could feel empathic concern for her. However, because the emotional expression was so blank, my empathic reaction was not as strong as one might expect in such circumstances.

The theme of wanting to take things home dominated the remainder of the interview. She left the room much as she had come, in a striding gait and with little emotional expression.

COMMENTS ON FIRST INTERVIEW

My impression was that Molly was a physically and neurologically intact 4½-year-old, as evidenced by her gross and fine motor coordination, use of language, and overall healthy appearance. There was a capacity for relating but it had little variation, richness, or depth and developed only to the point of expressions of affect hunger. She showed little warmth or intimacy, nor was she demanding or interested in a power struggle. Molly's capacity for relatedness seemed to be at a very concrete, early developmental level; she related like a somewhat sad 2- to 3-year-old.

The mood, as already described, seemed mostly depressed and constricted. The range of affect was quite narrow. Little was expressed beyond a mildly constricted or flattened quality and a degree of affect hunger around the themes of wanting to take things home. There was no affective demonstration of joy, curiosity, seductiveness, compassion, or empathy, nor were there signs of rage, protest, jealousy, or envy. In short, none of the age-appropriate affects were to be seen. The affects that were visible were well below age expectations—again, more like those of a constricted 2-year-old.

Molly showed a capacity to organize her themes. There were no overt fragmentations, no comments or themes from out of the blue. But there was little depth or richness to her thematic development; in other words, it was

95

shallow and concrete: Her shallow and impoverished thematic patterns were limited to asking if I had a lollipop, naming things in the room, standing in a corner and wanting to take off her shirt, and telling me the kinds of toys she liked and all the things she wanted to take home—themes that would be considered constricted even in a 2- to 2½-year-old.

The thematic sequence progressed from wanting something from me to an interest in exploring the room; the latter was followed first by inhibition, as she lodged herself in one quarter of the room, and then by a desire to show herself, which was quickly contradicted; finally she showed a desire for me to get to know her likes and dislikes of various toys (which also had the sense that she was telling me what she might like from me as a present). None of these themes was developed. Finally, near the end of the interview, she was telling me clearly that she wanted to take things home, and her statements were accompanied by a sense of affect hunger. The sequence suggests a little girl who feels quite hungry at a concrete level, who has concretized some of her human needs, and who is too frightened to let people know her. Although she wants to get close (by taking off her shirt), to reveal some of her needs, and to move into age-appropriate exhibitionistic themes, she becomes inhibited and returns to the theme of making concrete demands of the interviewer. One might hypothesize that strong conflicts are inhibiting a greater development in the sequence; perhaps conflicts around early primitive rage that accompanies some of this concretization, and around affect hunger. Because many questions remained after the first diagnostic interview, a second interview was conducted.

## Second Interview

In the second interview, Molly entered the playroom much as she had done in the first, demonstrating good gross and fine motor ability and a clear capacity for vocalization. She was not expressionless, however; there was an intense, depressed look on her face. Moreover, her eye contact was engaging rather than aloof. She also showed less initial tentativeness and demonstrated a capacity to communicate in a clear and organized way. After moving around to survey the room in a slightly more relaxed fashion than she had previously shown, Molly sat down on the beanbag, looked at me (although still maintaining the intense, depressed look on her face), and said, "If you think of scary things sometimes, you won't breathe." She then continued to talk almost nonstop for the remainder of the session while she sat on the beanbag or walked around. For the most part she kept eye contact with me in an intense, somewhat depressed look, but showed some emotional variation—a smile here, a look of bewilderment there.

At first she talked about robbers and killers hurting other people and herself, and then she stood up and pretended that she was a "rocket ship" that was going to "take off." She then came back to the theme of robbers and killers. When I asked her to say more about it, she replied that they could kill you by cutting you with a "knife," that they could take your "eyes out," that they could "break off in your stomach."

Then she made a reference to her younger brother. When I asked her about him, she quickly changed the subject and said, "At school no one likes me—they hate me." There followed a brief silence; then she said, "kill them." When I picked up on this phrase, her serious and intense look shifted to a mild smirk and she said, "but only pretend." She talked more about killing and being killed. After I made a summary comment, she said, "Family—they don't want me to die, they like me." She made a confused reference to not breathing again, but would not elaborate on it.

A few minutes later, while walking around and exploring the room, she commented, "I like my shape. I'm a girl. It's different from my brother because I have long hair." I offered a summary comment to encourage her to talk more about how she differed from her brother, but Molly only repeated what she had said and then shifted to playing with the crayons. She began scribbling and then spontaneously drew a "snake": a long oval shape with two legs sticking out the back, two arms sticking out the middle, and the face of a little girl (the sex was evidenced by the long hair around the face). As I took an interest in the drawing and began wondering aloud about it, she said something about it being "a snake that can't see females"; then her words became confused, but I heard, "it's poison." She scribbled around the image, then drew pictures of two or three more snakes and said spontaneously, "That's me. . . . If I look at it, I can't breathe." She abruptly put the drawings aside and, with a rather serious but inanimate look on her face, went to the other side of the room where she started naming objects.

As in the first interview, she wanted to know if there were things she could take home, such as a checkers set, some crayons, and paper cups and soap from the bathroom. I commented that she was telling me it was scary to look at a poisonous snake and that perhaps taking some things with her from the office would make her feel less afraid. Looking at me as though to take in the supplied connection, she simply reiterated her wish to have these things. While her affect as well as the sense of relatedness remained tense and depressed throughout, there was no disorganization or fragmentation to her themes. When the interview ended, she looked at me to say good-bye, and the expression on her face seemed to indicate a desire to return.

### COMMENTS ON SECOND INTERVIEW

During Molly's second interview, I again saw that neurological and physical functioning were at the age-appropriate level. With regard to her sense of relatedness, although she was a little more involved and somewhat more intimate than she had been during the first interview, she was still highly constricted. There was also constriction in the sense of rigidity and distance she created—despite the fact that she communicated a great deal. As before, her mood was tense and depressed, although she showed slightly more variation. Although her affect was again very constricted, there was a greater range than in the first interview. There were momentary smirks and smiles, and a few instances of something near to curiosity and pleasure in what she was doing. Her affect was not as flat; she showed a tense, more rigid quality this time, a sense of seriousness. The affect was also slightly richer and deeper than during the first interview.

Molly showed some anxiety during the second interview, particularly after drawing the snakes, when she went to the other side of the room and talked about the concrete objects she wanted to take home. There was no disorganization as a result of her anxiety, but neither was there a capacity to use anxiety as a signal and then return to its source, i.e., the drawings. Instead, she avoided the anxiety by almost pretending that the drawings were not there. There was some indication that the anxiety had to do with the themes of being poisonous or hurt.

Thematic organization was more in evidence during this interview than in the first. She showed a capacity to organize a number of themes—especially while drawing the snakes—and to integrate her communication around one specific theme that was obviously troubling her. There was greater depth and richness to the themes during this interview than during the first one: themes of hurting, cutting, taking eyes out, not being liked, hating, and being different from her brother, as well as feelings about poisonous, aggressive snakes. This thematic development was in only one dimension, however, that of aggression and hatred and their consequences. There was little thematic development in the other sectors that one would expect to see in a 4½-year-old. Thus, we saw a rich development along one dimension that was obviously of concern to her.

The thematic sequence revealed the nature of her drama. It progressed from fears of not breathing, to robbers and killers, to herself taking off like an explosive rocket ship, to eyes being cut out with knives, to others not liking her in school, to her family not wanting her to die, to being a girl and being interested in her own shape, to the poisonous snake who she says is herself, and then to a quick shift to her hunger to take concrete things home. All of these themes pointed to her preoccupation with aggression, bodily injuries, and death.

There was some indication that her emerging sexual identity was somewhat tied up in this frightening imagery, making it hard for her to feel comfortable about being a little girl. When she was too close to seeing herself as an aggressive, poisonous snake, she needed to switch to a more concrete mode and express her wish to take things home with her. Thus, at the point of anxiety when she came closest to her frightening self-image, she sought reassurances via a regressive, concrete tie to another person. Such a move suggests some fear of object loss. This fear seemed to be tremendous and close to the surface, actuated continuously by the aggressive themes. The pattern seems to be: she experiences a need; she feels "poisonous" and becomes fearful of loss; she then wants concrete objects as reassurances.

In this interview we see a number of age-appropriate areas of functioning (e.g., physical neurological, thematic organization, affect organization). But we also observe below age-appropriate functioning to a significant degree in her constrictions of affective and thematic range and depth, her style of relatedness, and her special thematic preoccupations.

### Case 10

*Interview*

Eddie, 3½ years old, was sitting next to his mother in the waiting room. I was impressed by his large face, glasses, and strong, scholarly look. He came and stood very close to me when I entered the waiting room, and I noticed that he walked in a comfortable, almost adamant manner with a slightly broadened gait. He quickly showed that his fine motor coordination was good by the way he held a pencil. Spontaneously, he took the drawings he had made from his mother and handed them to me as though he were doing it on her behalf. His voice initially had a slightly nasal, monotonous quality as he spoke in response to my introducing myself and asking his name.

He came into the office and immediately sat down and started scribbling on a piece of paper. He mentioned the words "Mommy" and "Daddy" and again told me his name. His drawing was mostly scribbles and lines; I asked what it was and he said, "Big body, big boy." He then found a doll, said, "I got dolly," and proceeded to point out and name the ears, arms, feet ("eats"), and mouth. He then started twisting the doll's arm and grimacing, as though he could understand it was hurting. "Ouch," he said. I commented empathically that it must hurt. He responded, "I like you. Hurt if I like, I like to, I like to." When I picked up on his use of the word "like," repeating things he likes, he said, "Throw him up, not hurt. Throw up high," and made reference to the doll's hands and mouth. He then grabbed a toy dog and again said, "Throw up. Play with doggy." He was playing in a less aggressive way with the toy dog and I commented, "Eddie seems to enjoy playing with the doggy." He responded "Yes," and hiccupped. He then stood up, almost wobbling, and played while standing.

At this point he seemed pensive. I commented that it seemed he had a picture of something in his mind. He said, "Mommy. Like to get Mommy for Daddy for office because like to." He then made a reference to needing money and wanting to count pennies. Then he came and stood almost on top of me, showing little facial expression and not looking in my direction. For a moment he stood still, but then he began shaking the toy dog and hitting its head. He gave a big yawn, then proceeded to say phrases: "I like to," "I got to you," "Mommy, doggy, and fun." He seemed to be moving even closer to me and to be getting uncomfortable, as though he wanted to relate but could not. He gave me a blank stare. I commented that he seemed to want to tell me something. He said, "Red point in mind."

There was very little variation in emotional tone or affect during this time. He was obviously struggling with something, to judge by the very serious look on his face. He began pulling on his fingers and said, "Getting yack off because I like to." He put his fingers in his mouth and wandered around the room, looking at me blankly. I commented that maybe he did not know what to do and suggested that perhaps he could tell me a little about Mommy and Daddy. He said, "Daddy and Mommy come here and I stay with babysitters . . . I like babysitters." When I asked him to tell me more about this, he became visibly anxious, put his hands on his neck, and said, "Mommy likes babysitters, that's all." He then went over to touch some of the toys but was tentative and seemed almost afraid to touch them. He referred to a duck and to Big Bird on

TV, commented that he had toys at home, and again positioned himself very near but not quite touching me.

Near the end of the interview I asked if he ever had dreams (describing what I meant), and he responded with, "Hurting, headache, go out." I asked him if his head hurt when he slept. He pointed to his head and repeated the word "headache" while standing very close to me in a rigid posture, with a kind of adamant, serious, joyless look on his face. When I ended the interview, he went out to the waiting room without much facial expression or attention to me, and he returned to his mother in a similar way.

COMMENTS

With the younger age groups, 2- to 3-year-olds, one generally relies more on the presenting symptoms and developmental history than on the clinical interview. Nevertheless, it will be instructive to review Eddie's performance to see what impressions can be gained from the interview data alone.

As indicated, the basic neurological and physical functioning seemed to be at an age-appropriate level. The mood had a general, almost unvaried, apprehensive quality. In terms of relatedness, an underlying intense hunger was expressed through physical closeness, but little actual emotional warmth or relatedness was manifested. Eddie's relatedness had a hungry yet impersonal quality. There was little range of affect. Although of an age-appropriate nature, his affects seemed contained and constrained: there was little show of joy or pleasure, and no actual outbursts of anger or protest accompanying the various thematic developments. Anxiety seemed to be generalized and related to overall concerns. On the whole, the interview had a mildly fragmented quality to it.

Thematic organization was not age-appropriate for a 3½-year-old in that there was no development of organized themes through play material or verbal expression. We saw a lot of pieces of communication in the context of some relatedness but also observed that the capacity for organized thematic communication was below age expectations. Likewise, there was little depth or richness to the themes. Most 3½-year-olds are able to communicate at an interactive and play level by integrating some verbalization with their play actions.

The thematic sequence proceeded as follows. We saw an initial interest in the body parts of a doll and in hurting the doll ("Ouch"); indications of liking the interviewer; and concerns with not hurting, with throwing things up, with wanting to "like" the toy dog or be close to it, with thinking about parents and "liking" or being "close to" Mommy, and with needing money. The themes evolved from concerns about body parts and hurtfulness, to ambivalence about hurting and liking (with liking being more related to Mommy, and hurting more related to Daddy), to concerns with accumulating money, to fun and hurting again (hitting the dog's head). The theme of moving close to and then away from me, suggesting ambivalence about accumulating or wanting things, followed. My attempt to help him express what was on his mind evoked the theme of the "red point," pulling things off his fingers, and putting fingers in his mouth. When asked about parents, he indicated that perhaps he gets the babysitters instead of his parents. When asked to talk about mother, he put his hands around his neck, again indicating some tension and anxiety, and said only, "Mommy likes babysitters." He related dreams to hurting and headaches. This thematic sequence, although disjointed, gives us some clues to his conflicts.

Notice that no single theme was developed to any depth. Being close to Mommy had something to do with choking or strangulation in an aggressive yet unrelated sense, perhaps indicating that more time was spent with the babysitter than with mother. After the choking theme, Eddie returned to an impersonal desire to accumulate (tentatively touching toys) as a way of handling the need for dependency. His response to dreams demonstrated additional concern with aggression and physical pain. In sum, we saw a child whose overall thematic capacity for organization, depth, and richness was well below age expectations.

Concerning the organization of affect around themes, Eddie seemed preoccupied with issues of ambivalence. He was ambivalent about being close to people, and both ambivalent and angry about hurting people. He hinted that he suffered "headaches" as a result of these conflicts. Overall, he was below age-appropriate functioning in terms of thematic affect organization, although he showed some depth in this respect.

In summary, there was some capacity for relatedness and for separation from mother. In the former, he was highly constricted, however, showing little warmth or sense of personal relatedness. Although his physical and neurological functioning were in the age-appropriate range, some aspects—such as mood stability—were slightly below age expectations. Other major functions, notably thematic organization and depth and richness of affect, were significantly below age expectations. In these areas he was functioning at about the 2- to 2½-year-old level. On the sole basis of this interview material, therefore, one would be concerned about uneven personality development in this child.

### Case 11

*Interview*

Jane was cute and well-built, although somewhat small for her age of 2 years, 11 months. As I entered the waiting room, she was standing, holding her mother's knee. She looked over in my direction and presented a kind of prepared look, as though she knew why she was there. Mother, after greeting me, quickly got together some toys that she had brought in a bag. (I had asked her to bring some of Janie's favorite toys.) They came into the office with me and sat down on the floor. As Jane walked into the room, she showed basically good gross motor coordination and gait. Mother took out some toys and suggested that Janie play with them. Janie looked over in my direction and around the room a bit with a solemn yet interested and curious expression. Although her facial expression was not animated, she projected some apprehension and tension. Mother also seemed slightly anxious, but promptly got down to business, offering the child a car and Lego blocks. Jane quickly began putting together some of the Legos, demonstrating excellent dexterity with her fingers and fine motor coordination.

As Jane began playing with the Legos, her mother began a running commentary, describing the child's activities. She looked directly at Jane as she spoke but also seemed to be doing it for my benefit. For instance, when Janie started rolling a toy car back and forth, mother said, "Oh, now you are playing with a car." Janie also talked as she played, saying, "I want the doll, give me the truck," etc. She was able to give a commentary of sorts as to what she was doing and to identify toys as she took them out—"That's a Lego, that's a cow," etc.

During this time Janie was clearly relating at an emotional level to both her mother and me, looking at mother and occasionally glancing in my direction. When she glanced at me, I smiled and, when I thought she was saying to me, "That's a cow," I commented, "Yes, it is," to make myself available for involvement in the play. However, it was also noticeable that there was little change in Janie's facial expression: while very involved in manipulating the toys and verbalizing what she was doing (I should mention her verbal capacity was at the level of short sentences), Janie showed

103

little range of affect or emotion. Instead, there was a constant apprehensive look to her face. There were, for example, no occasions when she broke into bright, excited, or gleeful smiles; nor were there any occasions when she became negativistic, stubborn, or seemingly angry.

Also noticeable was that Janie and her mother sat almost entirely in one spot. Janie moved to take things from the bag of toys but not to explore the room. She specifically did not show any interest in the toys that were in my toy closet, which was well within her eyesight. Finally, about 20 minutes into the interview, she looked over at my toys, and mother suggested that she might like to see what "Dr. Greenspan's toys were like." With that bit of encouragement, Janie got up and walked to the toy closet. She took out a block and said, "This is a block. I will build a house." Mother then helped her take out a number of blocks and Janie began piling them up. At this point she was showing a little greater interest and curiosity and some slight relaxation, although the affect still remained mildly apprehensive.

Again, in piling up the blocks, Jane showed a good capacity to concentrate and to focus on what she was doing. She took out toy cars and a truck, naming them as she did so. She then took out a gun, looked perplexed, and said, "What is this?" Mother said, "That's a gun," and then explained, "We don't have them at home." Except for helping each other with the materials, there was little direct interaction between mother and Jane around any of the play activities.

Soon Jane found a hand puppet in the form of a fish. She put it on her hand and said, "This is a fish. It's going to bite you, Mommy," then thrust it toward mother's face. Mother quickly drew back and, quickly and very aggressively taking the puppet away and onto her own hand, said, "It's going to bite *you.*" Then Jane took it back from her and mother, with a somewhat reflex response, extended her finger and let Jane pretend to bite it with the fish puppet. Subsequently Jane took out a duck puppet and played the same game. This time mother extended her finger in a more relaxed fashion. Again, mother withdrew rather abruptly when Jane went after her face. Although she did not take it away from Jane, she said, "The duck is going to bite *you.*"

Mother seemed interested in evolving some interactive play with Jane around this theme of the fish or duck biting her, but only to a slight degree. She did not take advantage of this interactive sequence to build on it by developing any associations or story line. For example, she did not say, "The duck must be hungry." There was also a mildly apprehensive look on mother's face during this more aggressive play. Jane put down the duck on her own after playing with it for a few minutes and then returned to removing items from the toy cabinet and naming them. She did this with a fairly comfortable, curious quality, although again she showed little joy or pleasure.

Shortly thereafter, Jane went back to sit on the floor with her own toys. Mother suggested that she show me her newest game, which was a small magnetized chalkboard with letters that attached to it. Jane took out the chalk and showed me that she could draw some lines. I then sat down on the floor and made myself available to her on a more physically intimate level. Jane initially responded to this by standing up behind her mother as though mildly apprehensive. After a minute or two of this she was able to come back and sit down next to me and show me how she could take the chalk and draw a line. I then drew a circle and asked her if she could copy that. She was able to do a fairly decent circle with only one side of it drawn more like a square. I then drew an X and she copied it, but drew just a single line. Mother suggested that she show me the letters, and Jane found the letter A, saying, "Abbey."

Mother, for the first time showing a truly joyful smile, said, "I didn't know you could do that." Mother explained to me that Abbey was Jane's sister's name. Jane then went on to name other letters, being able to do so on her own about 70 percent of the time with mother helping her about 30 percent of the time. Mother seemed proud, but indicated she had worked with Jane on this and was well aware that she could name these letters. What surprised her was that Jane could find the letter that matched the brother's name. As Jane was naming the letters, I too demonstrated pride and said things like, "That's terrific." Jane looked up at me, acknowledging the compliment, and then busily went back to name some more. Here again, however, she showed few signs of overt pleasure but instead maintained her chronic apprehensiveness.

During this phase of the activity with mother, Jane and me sitting together, the interaction was probably as comfortable as possible. In other words, even though Jane was mildly apprehensive and mother was busy encouraging her to name the letters, there was some sense of underlying relaxation. Subjectively, I felt that Jane was then probably as relaxed with me as she gets with most people, even though she had been with me only about 40 minutes at that point.

The interview continued in this vein until I suggested that we would have to stop in a minute. Jane took in those directions, and she helped mother put the letters and toys back in their places. During this time Jane was able to make good eye contact with me, accompanying her apprehensive look with a smile. After putting the toys away, mother got Jane's coat on and they prepared to leave. Jane was able to look at me and say good-bye as mother and I arranged another appointment before they left.

### COMMENTS

Jane demonstrated that her overall physical and neurological status was within age-appropriate guidelines. Although on the small side, she was physically well-built and well-proportioned. She had good gross and fine motor coordination, could formulate her words clearly and talk in sentences, and showed an excellent capacity to name items and letters. Her capacity to name the letters was probably a bit above age expectations, as was the capacity to match the appropriate letter with her sister's first name.

With respect to her relatedness, there was clearly a capacity for human relatedness, as demonstrated in the waiting room when she had her hand on mother's leg. For an almost-3-year-old, perhaps this showed a desire to be especially close to mother and to forgo the curiosity and explorative activities one might expect. She also clearly showed a capacity to relate to me by making immediate eye contact and acknowledging my presence even when she was playing with mother on the floor and I was sitting in my chair. This capacity was also demonstrated by her frequent glances at me and by including both mother and me when she was talking or naming things, even though it was also clear that the relatedness to me was more indirect.

Once I sat down and joined them on the floor, there was a sense of three people relating to one another and Jane was able to interact with me, follow my instructions, and look at me. There was a sense of warmth that came through in spite of the apprehensiveness. This quality of warmth should not be underestimated, as it demonstrated that her capacity for human relatedness was well founded. I would speculate, however—more by way of inference than by observation—that there is some restriction in the range of affect in her relatedness as well as in her sense of exploration, the latter evidenced especially by the extent to which she stayed close to mother during most of the time in the playroom.

Her mood, as reported, had an apprehensive and slightly anxious quality throughout the session. Even at the end, when warmth and relaxation came through a bit, there was no general sense of relaxation. There was very little variation in the mood, which overall seemed stable.

Constriction seemed to be present in the range of affects. There was the mild apprehension, only a slight show of curiosity and interest, and little genuinely gleeful happiness. Although there were some mild signs of aggressiveness, there was no accompanying affect. For example, when Jane tried to bite her mother's nose and finger with the hand puppets, she always did so with the same apprehensive and nervous look on her face rather than with a gleeful playfulness, an out-of-control belligerence, or a hostile negativism. In fact, none of these affect ranges were present during the interview. At no time was the affect inappropriate to the theme she was developing, however, and there was an overall sense of connectedness and warmth, as reported above. Her persistently apprehensive affect was not shallow in terms of connectedness and warmth.

There were no abrupt shifts or disorganizations during the interview stemming from anxiety. Generally, she maintained her focus on each play theme until she seemed to want to shift. That anxiety might have been present was indicated by her chronically apprehensive, nervous quality and by her need to stay physically closer to mother than one might expect of a child her age—perhaps indicative of an underlying separation anxiety. There were also some indications that mother had difficulty handling Janie's aggression, as when mother quickly turned the table with the hand puppets, saying, "It's going to bite *you.*" Perhaps such a response signifies mother's underlying fear of being attacked. Again, the above comments are speculations based more on inference than on direct observations.

Jane seemed capable of developing organized themes in little islands of play; for example, when she took out the toys, there was the theme of naming things and exploration. Then there were the themes of building the house and showing how she could name letters. Within each "thematic island" she was focused, organized, and cohesive, but she lacked the age-appropriate capacity for developing depth or richness. One would expect a 2½- to 3-year-old to show greater interconnectedness between the different islands, perhaps beginning a story with cars, developing it with the puppets, and then shifting to drawing.

With Jane, the depth and richness of the themes were at a fairly superficial level, more like that seen in a 2-year-old. With the exceptions of building the house and the mildly aggressive interaction with mother, Jane merely described things and materials. During the course of a 50-minute session, one would expect a child her age to show a greater capacity for symbolic elaboration and interaction, in contrast to symbolic description. Essentially, she showed that she could describe things in symbolic form by putting words to them, but she did not show the capacity to integrate organized fantasies, which one would expect if she were less apprehensive and anxious.

The sequence of themes was also confined to the descriptive level, except for the very interesting sequence where Jane twice used the hand puppets to attack mother and, in the first such attempt, mother quickly took the puppet from her and attacked back. Mother's response was perhaps quite telling: not only was it the only interactive theme but it was also the only time when both showed some hint of affect over and above the shared apprehensive quality.

With regard to my subjective reactions, I was impressed with the fact that mother worked so steadily and diligently with Jane and, at the nonaffective level, seemed very responsive to what Jane was doing. She picked up on and reverbalized each of Jane's communications as well as trying to help her construct a "bigger Lego set," build a house, name letters, and so forth. There was a kind of obsessive but very interested and hardworking quality to mother. At the same time, I was as impressed with mother's lack of affect range as I was with Jane's.

Nevertheless, I felt more relaxed and involved, almost like a member of the family, when I sat with them on the floor. It was this feeling that suggested to me that I was probably seeing as much relaxation as this dyad was able to achieve; it also opened a glimpse into the deeper underpinnings of warmth that existed between Jane and her mother, which were perhaps hampered by the chronic apprehension and anxiety they seemed to share. My reaction to mother quickly turning the tables when Jane, in a not terribly belligerent way, attempted to attack her was that mother's quick trigger may be the way she responds to any assertiveness or aggression from Jane.

In sum, Jane was functioning at an age-appropriate level except in terms of the depth and richness of both her affects and her thematic development. It should be pointed out, however, that both child and mother showed considerable strength in their abilities to focus and concentrate on the task at hand.

# Chapter 5

# Conducting the Interview

The purpose of the diagnostic interview can be stated simply—to learn as much as possible about the child. The interviewer's basic task, therefore, is to create a setting that maximizes the amount of information that can be observed. As you conduct the interview, ask yourself what you can do to create a richer learning experience, in particular, what would evoke more data relevant to the categories that we have been discussing or to other categories that you may have constructed. A subsidiary goal is to establish rapport with the child so he or she will not feel frightened about returning for future visits if treatment or further diagnostic sessions are indicated. Let us begin with some general perspectives and principles and then talk about the opening phase, the middle phase, and the ending phase of the interview.

Training yourself to be a skillful observer is essential to the conduct of a successful interview. Related to this is evolving a personally comfortable style. There are two basic approaches—the structured and the unstructured interview. Briefly, the structured interview consists of using techniques that direct the child toward certain play materials and then asking certain questions. An older child may be asked about his or her family, while a younger child may be asked to fill in the endings of certain stories.

Many of you are familiar with the "baby bird" story: the interviewer starts it by saying that a baby bird falls out of the nest, and the child is asked to finish the story. Another well-known example begins with the question: If you had three wishes, what would they be? In other words, as in sentence-completion tests, you start the child off with certain ambiguous or semidirected stimuli and the child is asked to complete them.

You may also structure the interview with devices of your own, for example, greeting the child in a certain way or posing a question about dreams. Whatever structure you employ, however, it is important to bear in mind that the child is responding to what you are doing, and you must observe and understand his or her reaction in this context. As you gain experience with many children, you will get a sense of the average range of expectable responses to the structured elements you employ. You will also learn to understand individual differences in response to the kinds of issues that you may raise.

The unstructured interview, in contrast to the above approach, follows the basic concept that the less you intrude, the more the child will tell you. I favor the unstructured approach because I think it creates more of a learning opportunity. Structure tends to contaminate your observations and makes it hard to know how much of what is going on is a product of what you are doing and how much is what the child is bringing to the situation. For a variety of reasons that are not altogether clear, most children will, if given the chance, let you know what is going on in their personality— both structurally, in terms of how well they can handle reality testing, impulse control, and the like, and experientially, in terms of thoughts, fantasies, and feelings.

Your primary interest, I need hardly add, lies in observing whatever material the child is willing to share with you. The advantage of the unstructured interview is that it allows children to tell their stories in their own way, which is equivalent to saying that it allows children to put their own structure on the situation. There will be ample opportunity to get responses to structured stimuli via psychological testing and discussions with parents and teachers. The Thematic Apperception Test (TAT) and the Rorschach provide "standard" stimuli and have been given to tens of thousands of children of all ages, so that the norms are well-established. Such tests yield far more refined results than those obtainable from structured interviews.

Although an unstructured interview may seem to allow more potential for making what you may consider mistakes, you must realize that there is no such thing as a wrong move unless you alienate the child and family so completely that they will not participate in the evaluation or treatment. Every move, whether strategically good or bad, leads to a reaction on the part of the child. If you observe the nature of that reaction, then you are using it constructively in that child's interest. The remainder of this chapter will explain how to conduct an unstructured interview.

Two general principles for the clinician's conduct during the interview will be suggested: (1) the clinician must tolerate his or her own discomfort as well as that of the patient to permit the full extent of the psychopathology to emerge, and (2) the clinician should observe continually in all the categories described in Chapter 2.

The specific principles for the beginning, middle, and end of the interview will also be suggested, including: (1) During the initial phase, to be warm, accepting, but not too seductive or charming in order to permit patients to show you (with minimal interference from you) how they begin a new relationship and what their own perceptions or anticipations are for this new experience (e.g., expecting to be exploited and humiliated, stuck with needles, filled up with good candy and cake, sexually seduced, competed with). (2) During the middle phase of the interview, to facilitate patients' associative trends and to observe the organization, depth, richness, and sequence of affects, themes, sense of relatedness, mood, etc. Comments from the perspective of the patient's ego and sense of mastery may be useful with regard to his or her initial perception of the meaning of the interview (especially if it is fearful) as well as in dealing with conflicts and/or themes or affects that may emerge during the middle phase of the interview. In essence, the goal of the middle phase is to help patients permit you "to get to know them," and to observe this process carefully, noting how much patients facilitate the goal on their own and how they use your help (e.g., ignore your comments, get disorganized, or use your comments to enrich their associative trends both affectively and thematically). (3) During the latter phase of the interview, to observe how patients prepare for and deal with separation from you and with your comments on relevant themes, and —most important—how they deal with highly stressful, potentially frightening affects that might undermine future diagnostic or therapeutic work. The goal here is to help patients consolidate, from the perspective of their ego or mastery, a sense of a unique and useful experience.

Before elaborating the basic principles, I want to make a suggestion: use notepaper with columns drawn for each category to facilitate your task of maximum observation; you can then enter your observations in the appropriate columns as the interview progresses. Another method is to make notes that give a running description of the interview, keeping the categories in the back of your mind. After several interviews, observing in all the categories becomes almost automatic. With practice it becomes easy to reconstruct the interview afterwards.

Now to the basic principles. To become a good, noninterfering observer, you must follow the principle of tolerating discomfort in the child as well as in yourself. You are not going to be able to diagnose psychopathology unless you permit the child to show it to you. If a child shows anxiety (e.g., by disrupting play or crying) and you move in too quickly to support him rather than letting him play it out for you, you will not observe how well he can handle it on his own. Of course, you always have to make a clinical judgment in these areas. If a child becomes very disorganized and frightened, you may have to move in and help him restructure his world. Symbolically speaking, you do not want the child to hurt once you have observed the nature of the psychopathology. However, you do want to observe fully just how deep and intense that psychopathology is, and this you cannot do if you close off the behavior prematurely.

When the time has come to be supportive, it is best to comment on the behavior rather than gloss over the child's difficulty and shift attention away from it. For example, it is important for 4- and 5-year-olds to feel that you are not only interested in what they tell you but also that you are not frightened by it. When you make a statement in an area of difficulty, children are often greatly relieved to know that finally they have met someone who is not frightened by what frightens them. Although a child may be too afraid to talk about a problem directly in the first interview, he or she will at least know that you are ready to listen.

As for our own discomfort, there are certain kinds of behavior that cause anxiety in most of us, no matter how experienced we are—for example, primitive disorganized behavior. We like nice garden-variety neurotic conflicts that may be similar to our own and therefore easy to understand. But we dislike and will tend to cut off primitive behavior, particularly if it touches on something in our own unconscious. Often we do not recognize our own anxiety as such. Instead, we may experience a first-level defense against it, which might very well be the thought, "This child is getting too disorganized. I'd better structure the interview for him." What one really may be thinking is, "His behavior or feelings make me too disorganized. I had better structure the interview for myself." If, in the first diagnostic interview, you feel the need to move in very quickly, your first thought should be, am I taking care of myself or am I taking care of this child? Far more than adults, children possess a marvelous talent for touching on our own sensitive areas, probably because they wear their conflicts much more on their sleeve, so to speak. With children, our own countertransference or reaction tendencies will be much more easily elicited. If you find yourself becoming uncomfortable, it is best to say nothing, observe what happens for at least a few minutes, and note any fantasies of your own that come to mind.

The next principle is the one I have been elaborating all along, that is, follow the communications of the child—not only the content of the themes but also the associative trends from the viewpoint of the child's relatedness, emotional tone, and affects over time. By following such communications closely, you will be able to support their development while at the same time being available to the child when needed. This principle will be further exemplified as the different phases of the interview are discussed below.

The first phase of the interview begins in the waiting room. Your first observations are of the child with his parents; notice their spatial relationship and interactions. Then, as discussed in Chapter 2, before approaching the parents or child, pause for a moment and get your first impressions of the child, noticing such things as physical makeup, coordination, gross and fine motor activity, and sensory motor functioning. Observe how the child responds to mother and other family members, as well as to other people in the room. You may even have an opportunity to see affects and activities that give you information for some of the other categories.

For example, you may begin to see a range of emotion as the child navigates the room, or to get a sense of the child's overall mood. You may observe a moment of stress between the child and mother if the child is disobedient. This interaction will allow you to observe how the child handles anxiety. If the child is playing alone or with another person you can even see something of his or her thematic organization and range. Clearly, the observations in those first few minutes in the waiting room need to be supplemented with additional material from the interview, but they can provide you with an initial impression of the child's status in many of the developmental categories and with a preliminary intuitive feeling for the child.

As for beginning your interaction, it is preferable to make contact with the child before doing so with the parents if the child seems available to you. In this way, the child begins to understand that you are mainly interested in getting to know him or her. After your greeting, simply ask the child to come with you to the playroom. Here again, there will be some interesting behavior to observe as the child begins relating to you as a new person. If you just offer them your person without any seductive, sugar-coated trimmings, most healthy children will show some trepidation, some mild apprehension, some mild caution, yet a trusting-enough attitude to come along with you because they usually have some sense about why they are there. If, on the other hand, you approach the child with cookies or candies, you will not get a picture of the ordinary way this particular child responds to a new person.

Some children may run along ahead of you when you point to the room. Others will lag along a few feet behind you. If the child is very young, you may offer your hand. You will get an intuitive sense of when to do that. Other children may refuse to leave mother, and your first diagnostic task may be how to deal with the child who is holding onto mother and refusing to separate. In some such cases you may want to take a step back and see what mother or father does. Some parental figures will grab little Sally, saying, "You've got to go into the room, you are embarrassing me," and then take the child by the arm and drag her into the room. Although you feel motivated to interfere because you think the parents are being brutal to the child, I think you are wiser to wait and see how the parent deals with the child and how the child deals with the parent: Does the child provoke the mother, for instance, or is it the other way around? In any case, you can assume that if the parent behaves that way here, he or she does so everywhere. At a certain point you may want to do something to ease the situation, but it is useful to get the natural picture first. Do not let your own anxiety interfere with your observing the situation for a short time.

I usually have the playroom set up with toys or games appropriate to the child's age so that the room is somewhat organized when the youngster enters. I welcome children with a warm hello and a smile and then let them make the first move. Some people believe in giving candy to establish a bond between the therapist and child; however, I regard this as a spurious gift because the therapist has something much better—professional skill—to

114

offer. Once the child senses this, he or she will attach to the therapist in a far more profound way than through a gift of candy. I do not ask, "Do you know why you are here?" because it limits the potential range of responses the child may show. For instance, in response to this direct question the following dialogue may ensue.

C: Because my mother said I should come.
T: Why did your mother say you should come?
C: I don't know.
T: Oh, come on, you know.
C: No, I don't know.
T: Oh, come on, your mother must have told you something.
C: Well, it has something to do with school. I don't do well in school.
T: Why don't you do well in school?
C: Well, I don't know and I am not going to tell you!

This is not an uncharacteristic interview with a child. Although there is nothing wrong with having such an exchange, you do not learn as much as you would if you allowed the child to tell you in his own way (and he will) why he thinks he is there.

With reference to the situation you and the child are about to share, you can be sure that he has a preconceived notion of why he is there and how he is going to handle it. If you explain too quickly who you are, how long you are going to be together, etc., you will not learn what the child's ideas are. Similarly, although you may have the benefit of the child's history from the parents, you should not confront the child with this material, for it may elicit the response, "If that is what they told you, why don't you talk to them about it." However, you certainly should use the information (symptoms) related by the parents as one perspective from which to observe the child. For example, if the parents have told you that the child is stealing, you might watch for signs of emotional hunger—that is, does the child steal in order to "fill himself up"—or for signs of anger—does the child steal in retaliation? You might also be alert to sneaky or tricky maneuvers, a derivation of stealing.

Once the child has shared with you as many of his perceptions as he is able to, you should give him some feedback on what he has told you to show that you understand. You can also correct any distortions by offering your understanding of his concerns, and you can set out certain terms of your relationship, such as how long you will be together on this occasion and whether you will be seeing him again. Depending on the child's age, you may want to describe how you see the goals of your time together. Once again, you will do well to wait until you have heard the child express his or her goals before stating your own (which should be explained in a context the child will understand). For instance, if a child says that he expects something special, you can explain, "Although I know you want some cake and candy from me, I'm going to try and help you in a different way." That way the child will know that he or she has been heard and understood.

At this point you may also want to tell the child the rules of the playroom —typically, that he is free to play, and say and do anything he wants, but he cannot break anything or hurt either you or himself. Laying down the rules of the playroom often gives the youngster a sense of freedom. Some children do not appear to need this explanation, as if they intuitively know the rules. Others appear to be frozen until you give them permission to explore, and still others immediately act aggressively. Again, do not explain the rules until you have seen how the child reacts to the room, otherwise you will miss an important piece of information about the child's personality.

The ambiguity present in the first few minutes is almost always an occasion of learning. For instance, one child in that first moment of anxiety looked around the room and asked if there was a tape recorder, a specific concern I might not have heard if I had intruded too quickly.

Another child came in and lay face down on the couch. Waiting to see what he would do, I felt that he was telling me something. Did he want to be in analysis (maybe he has a parent in analysis), was it a sign of dependency, was he terribly tired, or was fear causing him to bury his head like an ostrich? After some moments I described to him what he was doing and wondered if he could tell me what he was feeling about it. It evolved later in the interview that something frightening had happened to him just before the interview. From his behavior, I saw one of the ways he deals with frightening experiences.

Another child, a 9-year-old, began by sitting down in a mature way and telling me that his mother had brought him because he was fighting with his little sister. I got the feeling from his demeanor that he was waiting for something. I commented on this and he said, "Yes, I'm waiting for my shot. When you go to doctors, you get shots." He described this huge needle that I was going to use and went on to say that although his mother said I was

116

a different kind of doctor, not the kind that gave injections, he did not believe her. He still expected a huge shot and he expressed this with an air of excitement. Later on I commented that he had not seemed frightened by the idea of the needle, and this set him off into other areas of expectations that led to a picture of some of his conflicts.

With regard to children who are initially rigid and silent, suppressing your immediate urge to structure their activities will allow you to discover whether such children can begin something on their own. The following examples illustrate this.

A bright 7-year-old came in, sat down on my couch, and looked at me. I looked at him. I let that go on for maybe 30 seconds, which is very long in that situation. Most people would tolerate no more than 5 or 10 seconds before moving in to structure the situation and make it more comfortable. This particular child seemed to become more frozen with anxiety as time went on. When I saw his discomfort growing and realized that he was only going to get more rigid, I ended the silence. I had observed what I wanted to know; that is, I learned that he could not overcome his anxiety, and thus began structuring the situation. By tolerating his discomfort and my own, I learned that he could not take charge, so to speak.

Another child started out exactly the same way, seemingly frozen, but after about 20 seconds she made a comment about the room, relating it to her own house. She continued to make herself comfortable by associating back and forth, essentially saying that being there with me was not all that unfamiliar and frightening to her. Obviously it *is* a new and frightening situation, and this child was demonstrating a tremendous coping capacity that spoke volumes to me about how she deals with a stressful situation.

With children like the one in the first example, I try to say something that picks up on what I think the child is feeling; or if I want to be more impersonal about it, I will say that people sometimes come here (to the interview room) and don't know what to make of the situation. To the silent boy, I said, "You're not sure what to think or say." He then made a few comments about the house we were in that made him feel a little more relaxed. That got him grounded and he said, "I don't know why I'm here or what I'm supposed to do." He wanted me to give him direction.

Now most 7-year-olds would be opening up the toy closet, looking around the room, exploring the range of options available to them. Therefore, with this particular child I did not immediately accept that he did not know what to do. I said, "You have no idea at all?" and continued with

117

comments about how it feels to be in a strange place with no idea why you are there and what his parents may have told him. Once I broached the latter issue with him, he somewhat reluctantly said, "Well, you're a doctor who talks about feelings." Then he slowly revealed to me that his parents had told him that he was coming to talk about feelings and that they had already talked to me; he added that he felt "strange" about his own feelings. Then we were off and running, but it had taken a good 10 minutes of exploration before he was willing to tell me that he had some understanding —which was fairly profound—of why he was there.

His initial feeling of strangeness, communicated through silence, was indeed where *he* wanted to begin. In the end, I did not have to tell him much of anything. All I had to do was confirm his understanding of the situation. He showed me he was a boy who holds back, who uses a passive stance to life as a way of dealing with a whole variety of issues. (In fact, this was one of the problems his parents were concerned about, that their bright child was not doing well in school and had trouble asserting himself.) I was able to see that behind the passive stance there was a considerable reservoir. Once he got started, he was able to develop well-organized themes and a sense of relatedness to me. He showed me that his passive stance was not a rigid defense covering up some major defects in core personality functioning, for example. I saw that this was a child with many assets who was troubled by "strange feelings."

With respect to making comments, warm affect is important: *what* you say is not as crucial as *how* you say it. Above all, in the first few minutes do not begin steering the child in a particular direction. Leave him free to choose an initial theme. You do want to indicate your understanding of his feeling, to give him some feedback on what he has told you, but you do not want to lead him with your comment. By making a supportive comment you are not only telling the child what he is doing, you are showing him what you have to offer. With a challenging child, such as one who is rigid, it is important not to be too easy on him, otherwise you will not learn the answer to some of the difficult differential diagnostic questions.

For example, if you are seductive and appealing, even a seriously depressed child will respond by giving you all sorts of interesting dynamic material. This may help you understand her conflicts but, in so behaving, you may miss the fact that she is depressed or basically negativistic. You may indeed want to use charm at some point in the treatment relationship where it may have particular value in helping the child understand something or ally with you in the observing function. Until such time, however, your comments should be warmly empathic, but not too much so, and never cold or remote, for either extreme will contaminate the child's reaction.

The extreme opposite to the rigid child is the child who is uncontrollable. Here you have to decide when to step in. Let us say you are 5 minutes into the interview and the child is smashing things and beginning to kick you. What you do partly depends on what you are willing to tolerate. Some therapists will tolerate some breakage but will physically try to control the child if they are hit. Others will let the child continue through the whole session in order to see at what point the child will finally feel enough involvement to be able to control himself.

If you feel physical restraint is required, you can try holding the child as you make comments in an effort to calm him or her. You may become exhausted and have to call for help. You want to see just what it takes to help this child get organized: will two—or even three—adults in the room be sufficient; will bringing in the parents do it; or will the child organize himself without help after some moments? I would use the situation to learn about the child and not assume after two or three outbursts that some sort of restraint is necessary. Such a decision is a matter of personal style. Some people are unwilling to risk exhaustion or being hurt.

Some of you may find that your own personality is such that difficult children, particularly aggressive ones, tend to get organized in your presence and will not challenge your authority. Others may find that, on the contrary, such children challenge you repeatedly. Some of you may be better with passive children. A frightened and passive child, seeing a person who conveys an image of authority, may withdraw for most of the session. With a less imposing figure, a gentler or more soft-spoken person, that same child may be willing to engage in a dialogue. It is important to know your own baseline and the kinds of reactions that you tend to induce.

You also should know yourself well enough to know the responses certain kinds of children evoke in you. All of us will have different reactions to the same child, and it is important to learn what yours are likely to be. If you are uncomfortable with aggression, you may react paradoxically with sympathy and pity toward aggressive children. Although you may work well therapeutically with them, it is important to know that your idiosyncratic reaction to these aggressive children is to feel extraordinarily "maternal." You want to make them "nice" children, to overlook or excuse their aggressiveness. You see only the needy and deprived side rather than seeing this together with the aggressive side. The point is not that you should change your reaction but rather that you should learn how to use it. Then it becomes another instrument, another source of information for you.

In summary, during the first phase of the interview you should be concerned with the child communicating why he is there, how he views you, and how he understands the situation. While this part of the child's story is unfolding, it is important not to direct his thoughts or activities. The comments you make during the first phase of the interview should show your supportive understanding of the child's concerns. They should clarify the goals of the session once the child has shared his notions of why he is seeing you, and they should serve to establish a working relationship between you and the child, that is, to show the child that you can understand and help him.

The middle phase of the interview offers excellent opportunities to observe in all the categories discussed in Chapter 2. By this time the child will have evinced some predominant affects, begun to form some kind of relationship with you, shown you an overall emotional tone, and developed a theme which probably had some disruptions in it, allowing you the opportunity to see the child handle anxiety. You will be noting the thematic sequences, which help to create linkages, as well as the richness, depth, and age-appropriateness of the themes, which tell you something about the structural capacities of the child's personality. During this time, it is also important to note your own subjective reactions and fantasies.

The major goal of the middle phase of the interview is to facilitate the unfolding of the child's story. You want to follow his leads and help him make associative links when his own defenses create a block. The preconscious and unconscious elements of the story will emerge in terms of the sequence as the child moves from theme to theme. The job of the diagnostician is to make sense of what may seem like a series of disjointed themes. By listening with a sensitive ear, one can follow the trend of associations. With an adult this is done through understanding a series of statements; with a child it is achieved by observing the evolution of play, words, affect, and relatedness to you throughout the interview.

After you get a picture of how well the child can organize themes, you can make comments that help the child find transition points or linkages. Basically, your comments should try to play back the theme that the child has presented. It may be quite difficult at times to pinpoint the theme because of the complex ways in which children communicate: the meanings

120

conveyed through play, body posture, and style of relating can be exceedingly subtle. Your comments should also focus on whatever category seems most immediate or relevant to a particular child. With some children you may want to comment on the affect, for example, "It seems like people feel angry a lot." Or you may want to comment on the story line, for example, "It seems like every time people get close, they lose the people that they care for." Let us say the child is dealing with jealousy and is markedly anxious and tense. A helpful comment might be: "You know, when people want a lot and there is only a little bit, sometimes people get very nervous and tense." In this case your comment focused on the content and affect.

Because our categories of observation are all integral parts of a child's internal economy—all parts of the way she experiences her world—you cannot go too far off the mark no matter which category you choose to emphasize. Still, if you are able to comment on the area of most intense involvement, the child will probably respond better and develop her communications more fully and richly. Make your comments curious rather than provocative. Even a "Tell me more about that" will help. In general, if a child is stuck (i.e., repetitive) at the level of content, you may want to highlight the affect, and vice versa.

When making comments, it is especially important to be aware of another general principle, that is, try not to ask questions. Put whatever you need to say in the form of a declarative statement. If a child is behaving aggressively toward you, instead of asking, "Are you angry with me?" or "Do you tend to get angry?" say to him or her, "It seems that you are angry," "You are trying to hurt me," and so on. Making such statements also suggests to the child that putting things into words is another way of expressing thoughts and feelings. This gives the child another option, one with more flexibility than wordless action or internal fantasy.

It is important to stay away from comments directly oriented toward increasing any fearful, instinctually laden impulses you may observe. Although you should recognize the child's frightening thoughts and feelings, stay on the side of the child that is trying to master her fears. Let us say a child is nearly overwhelmed with all kinds of instinctually laden wishes and fears of what might happen, but consciously feels panicked and confused. To say, "This must be a confusing situation," is to address the conscious part of her ego, the side of her personality that actively processes experience. Even this comment may be threatening, however. The child may be one who is easily humiliated; she may respond by showing you how

121

strong she is, saying, "No, I never get confused about anything." Then you will recover quickly by saying, "It seems as though it's best to be in control of things. You like to be on top of things." Here, instead of using charged phrases such as, "You don't like to be helpless . . . passive . . . humiliated," you say, "You like to be in charge of things . . . in control." Usually the child will agree with you. At first you will not know which are the charged words, but after you make some initial comments, you will begin to sense which words to stay away from, and will be better equipped to phrase supportive comments.

For example, suppose a child tells you about other children on the block who like to beat up people, then suddenly goes silent and starts spinning around and moving rhythmically. You see the child's anxiety has gotten high, causing her to regress to rhythmical body movements. At that point you might say, "Gee, talking about people beating up other people is a scary kind of thing." Now that may either help the child to go on or she may choose not to tell you anything else about beating up people. She may switch to drawing or something else less affectively laden, and then come back to the theme of aggression later on. By pointing out to her that it is frightening to talk about angry feelings (she showed you how frightening she found it by switching to an autistic type of behavior pattern right after mentioning it), you are showing the child that you can understand and accept her concerns and that you know they are frightening; thus you are not siding solely with the drive component of her revelation. One does not say, "Tell me more about aggression," but instead sides in a balanced way with both the coping capacity and the affects and drives that cause anxiety.

Another example is provided by the child who gets caught up in repeatedly punching the Bobo doll and the beanbag after taking off the doll's clothing. After you have observed how he integrates the theme of punching and anger with other aspects of the playroom, as well as how he relates to you and what kind of affects are generated, you might move in and say something quite simple, e.g., "You know, punching and taking off clothes both seem to be very important to you." With this comment you may help the child extend his associations, thereby getting a picture of his willingness to deepen and enrich his themes.

At some point around the middle of the interview, if you feel you have a sense of what the child is communicating, it is sometimes helpful to pull together a number of elements into what might be called an "ego-related clarification" (not synonymous with an interpretation). Such a clarifying statement would include the affects that are manifested, the key thematic material accompanying these affects, and the way the child is dealing with these elements. The child's reaction to the clarification can teach you a good deal about how he organizes his thinking and deals with conflict-ridden material.

As with simpler comments, the manner in which the clarification is offered is important to its success. The clarification should side with the child's ego rather than trying to interpret deep unconscious longings, hungers, or aggressive feelings. You should always maintain a balance, seeing the coping capacity as well as the underlying wishes and fears, but have that balance lean toward the child's strengths.

For example, suppose that during the first half of the interview the child has demonstrated anger, jealousy, and rage and shown little of the compassionate and empathic affects. Using dolls, he has been unfolding a story in which his schoolmates mistreat him and think they are better than he is. Later he plays out the same story with the toy animals and has a policeman step in to stop their fighting. He continues to repeat this theme in a controlled way without developing it further. You ask him to tell you more about the fighting, hoping that he will make the theme deeper and richer. Instead he replays it in a more obsessive way, showing you the issue of control.

You decide to make a clarification based on the affect and the story line. You say how important it is to be in control of things when people feel angry, hoping that the child will use the clarification to reach a deeper level of association. He becomes provocative and counterphobic, taking a gun and shooting darts at you. You make another clarification, again reflecting on his wishes, themes, and styles of coping: "Yes, sometimes when people feel unsure of being able to control their feelings, one way to deal with it is to attack." Reassured because he sees that you have understood him, the child now begins further exploration of the underlying issues, which I regard as a good prognostic sign for the child in treatment.

In all cases, you want to watch closely how a child responds to your clarifications. The behavior may be indirect; the child may move to another part of the room and start a new activity such as drawing. But while the child is drawing, you may suddenly realize that through this activity he or she is indeed telling you more about aggressive feelings or fears of separation. You see that the child has essentially taken in and integrated your comments and moved onto another plane, thus offering you a greater under-

standing of what is going on. The clarification has given the child a beginning sense of what therapy can be, a sense that a trained person can help
the child organize things in a way that he or she could not do alone.

At the midway point of the interview you will have done much of the
important work: observed how the child develops themes and relates to you,
noted where different affects are demonstrated, and so on. You have given
the child the opportunity to tell you what is on his mind and how he is
feeling about life in general, and you have made clarifications and watched
his reactions to them. With helpful comments from you as needed, continue
to observe how the child develops his story, all the while watching for
increasing depth and range in the seven categories.

As the end of the session nears, begin to summarize the important issues
the child has been communicating to you. Such comments, which convey
to the child the fact that your meeting will soon end, will allow you to see
how he deals with separation. Keep in mind that any shifts in behavior may
be related to the expected separation. Thus, a well-modulated child may
suddenly start being aggressive, and a somewhat withdrawn child may start
coming closer, even clinging to you. A child who has been quiet during most
of the interview may finally show a willingness to talk about feelings,
perhaps rousing your anxiety because you feel you must extend the interview time. However, you must realize that the child's very motive in opening up may be to keep you involved so that he does not have to leave. In
such a situation you might say, "Sometimes people feel like talking more
just when they are about to leave someone." This kind of comment will help
the child understand that part of his desire to open up to you is related to
his having to part from you. Later on, after you have seen the child several
times, you may want to make a comment about this behavior by saying
something like, "Here we are talking and you're telling me a lot of important things that I'm eager to hear more about, but I wonder how come
you're telling me about it now? Sometimes people do this just before they're
ready to leave, which makes it much harder to leave, because you've got
so much to talk about." In general, whatever the child's particular style, you
want first to help him understand that the end of the interview is coming
and then to make him aware of his reaction to the impending separation.

Near the end of the interview, with 5 or 10 minutes remaining, I often
ask some structured questions. Usually by that time the child has indicated
the nature of the family constellation. If he has not, I might ask him about

his family: "Tell me about . . ." Typically, I will get the first association—"Mommy, oh she's never home." Father—"He makes lots of money." Baby brother—"Takes away my toys." Sometimes you get a startling response. Father—"Oh, he kills people." "Tell me about that." "Oh, I was just kidding."

Often I ask the child if he ever has dreams—daydreams and night dreams—and a very high percentage tell me their dreams. Occasionally one hears an interesting dream that helps to support or refute hypotheses formed in the course of the interview. Depending on the time and on what else I have learned, I might ask a child about school or friends to hear first associations, or I might ask if the child has any questions he wants to ask me. I usually try to include the latter by saying, "You have told me a lot. Is there anything I can tell you?" Very often I get something interesting in response. Let me add, however, that concluding structured questions yield information of less value than what you gathered during the unstructured period of the interview.

The phases of an unstructured interview proceed as follows. In the initial phase the child communicates why he is there, and you clarify and support his feelings. In the middle phase, the child begins to get to know you better and to develop a relationship with you. Here, you observe the child in all the categories as his story unfolds, making helpful comments to further associative trends and synthesizing clarifications. The final phase, signifying "good-bye," shows how the child deals with separation. At this time, you may also wish to ask a few structured questions.

### Case Illustrations of the Technique of Conducting an Unstructured Interview

In order to illustrate the principles discussed above, we will now reconsider some thematic aspects of the initial, middle, and final phases of the clinical interviews presented in Chapter 4. It may prove useful to refer back to those interviews cited.

In the initial phase of the interview in Case 1, Doug finally reaches out with his "Hi" after some moments of paralyzing anxiety, then continues without reserve. Displaying some emotional hunger, he talks of his need for security (saving money) and his worries about illness. It is his choice to open the dialogue by letting the interviewer know that he is in distress and willing to reach out. Hints of deeper concerns also emerge as themes of physical damage are elaborated early in the interview, perhaps suggesting what Doug may be afraid of in developing a new relationship.

In the middle part of the interview we see the theme get more organized and the plot thicken. Doug talks about saving his money "to take care of future emergencies," then becomes concerned with "robbers and lazy bums" hurting people, stealing his money, and also perhaps hurting his brother. Here it is not clear who he is referring to as "robbers and lazy bums." Is it a part of him that would like to "rob others" and perhaps "hurt my brother," or is he expressing some potential worries about the interviewer? The interviewer could be the villain who would rob him and harm his brother. Perhaps he is referring to somebody else, or to a mixture of all of the above. In any event, we see conflict arising between his wish to be secure—to save and have plenty of money—and his fear of lazy bums, robbers, and other thieves who could hurt him.

The interviewer then makes a clarifying comment indirectly, by thinking out loud about robbers without trying to lead Doug in any particular direction—such as seeing himself, the interviewer, or family members as the robbers—because on his own Doug is developing this theme and its conflictual sides. Through tone of voice the interviewer's clarification is meant only to underline the concern. (Later on, perhaps in the treatment situation, one might make a more explicit clarification as the particular meaning Doug was elaborating became more understandable.)

It is also interesting to note how Doug moved into the last part of the interview. The prospect of separation evokes his underlying emotional hunger: he wants to continue playing games, to take things with him, and to be assured that he will be able to return. We observe that, instead of demonstrating overt anger as do some children who have a great deal of emotional hunger, Doug tries to reassure himself by taking a symbol of the interview home with him as well as by seeking assurances of the continuation of the sessions.

The interview with Joan in Case 3 further illustrates the characteristic progression of the unstructured interview. In the earliest part of the interview Joan reveals her interest in things sticking out (the Bobo's nose) and in breaking off what sticks out. Following this she becomes more structured, thereby perhaps indicating some anxiety about this interest. We might hypothesize that she is opening up her interview by saying that she herself is anxious about "sticking her neck out" in terms of what she will relate in this setting and that she is worried about being "broken off." In other words, she is anxious about what she feels to be her own tendency to open up and let things stick out. Or perhaps she is conveying the way she relates to others, that if they offer to get to know her, she is afraid she will break off what they extend. In the opening phase we may speculate but cannot know whether she is talking about herself or others or some combination. We do get a picture of how she perceives the situation: something is going to begin sticking out and then something may get broken off.

In the middle of the interview she starts to elaborate a conflict. She is concerned about the wolf pretending to be grandmother, and then becomes curious and suspicious about the mirrors on the wall. The interviewer comments that Little Red Ridinghood must have been scared and unsure about the world, and that she, Joan, must be unsure about what's happening in this situation, whether there are wolves around and what these mirrors mean. As will be recalled, after a moment of apprehension, after tearing off the paper she was drawing on, she began a theme with the policeman doll and flirted with the idea of dropping it out the window. The plot deepened with the scene of the dolls in the toilet. Through these developments as well as subsequent ones, Joan showed that she was able to use the clarification of a possible conflict she was experiencing to elaborate themes expressing her concerns in an extraordinarily rich and dramatic fashion.

Near the end of the interview Joan talks about a dream in which witches give out "bread with poison on it"; her father eats this bread and dies. After relating the dream, Joan puts a block under her dress, shows concern with the interviewer's note-taking, and relates how her mother stole "Hanukkah money" from her. There is a quality of emotional hunger at this point, as though she wants to go on and on about these various concerns. In response to the impending separation she might be saying, "I have a lot more to tell you about many scary things" and "I'm not sure how to understand this experience. Did somebody get poisoned, tricked, or have things stolen from her? I feel uneasy about my own body." Such expressions of fearful uncertainty about what happens in relationships with other people might be echoes of the stick-out–break-off theme heard at the beginning of the interview.

The Case 4 interview with Cathy is also instructive. She begins by setting up a family scene using the toilet as a chair, then says that she has to clean the toilet first. Her opening seems to be one of trying to discover what she may and may not do, or perhaps how much she may or may not regress

127

in the situation. In a sense she is saying, "Hello, how are you. What gives here? Is this a place where I have to be clean or can I be messy?" She gives a hint that this may be a general concern in her life, that this is how she greets a new situation.

This concern continues in a muted way throughout the opening phase as she begins to develop her themes. Later, during the middle phase, when she is playing with the salt and getting it all over everything, she mentions that her mother "wouldn't let me do that." Again perceiving an attitude of "should I or shouldn't I," "can I or can't I," the interviewer comments that Cathy might be concerned with rules, and how they differ between here and home. Cathy then becomes more expansive, sharing her fantasies of being aggressive with mother, although again showing the theme of doing and undoing: "I threw things at mother, no I didn't"; "I kick mother, no I don't." Nevertheless, Cathy shows more freedom after the clarification and eventually comes to the point where she not only talks about her mother and her concerns with bombs, but wants to confide "a secret about Mother throwing a hamburger at Daddy."

As the end of the hour approaches, after relating themes of aggression about monsters and scary doctors and then punching me in the arm, Cathy suddenly becomes very curious. She looks in drawers and pretends no one knows what she is doing, indicating some sneakiness. She says that she has "more stories" in a flirtatious, expansive manner. Thus we see her dealing with separation: continuing the development of her thematic concerns about what is permitted and what is not permitted; giving free vent to her underlying feelings, wishes, and interests; and also saying in effect, "I have much more to offer you." She leaves on a confident note. There is no emotional hunger, no anger, no expression of relief. Rather, a confident statement is made. She conveys that there is more to discover, lots of things and many people she is interested in. She also hints that she has something in her own private "drawers," i.e., her own stories, which leaves the interviewer with a feeling of curiosity.

Readers may find it useful to review the other interviews presented in Chapter 4 or interviews of their own in order to study how the different phases of the clinical interview evolve. By following the basic principles discussed earlier, that is, facilitating communication, tolerating discomfort, and maximizing observations, the diagnostician will be able to gather sufficiently rich data from any type of child. If the diagnostician is unable to observe what a child communicates, that does not mean that the child is in fact uncommunicative. Even the child who sits there for 45 minutes and refuses to utter a word tells you something profound. By making use of the observational framework presented in Chapter 2, in the context of the unstructured interview, you will find that it is impossible for a child to be either uninteresting or uninformative.

# Chapter 6

# Constructing a Formulation Based on a Developmental Approach

The clinician making assessments of children has available, in addition to the diagnostic interviews, various other types of relevant data. The results of psychological testing, the child's developmental history, assessments of family functioning as a whole as well as of individual family members—all are necessary to the diagnostic process. From the data of clinical interviews alone, however, one can deduce useful hypotheses which may then be refined and further developed in the light of information from the other sources. In this way the systematic observations made in the diagnostic interview can become the cornerstone of your assessment and diagnostic formulation. The question dealt with in this chapter is: What is the best approach to take in considering the observations and impressions gathered in interviewing the child? The approach I advocate here is a developmental one.

Using each of the observational categories we have been discussing—i.e., physical and neurological development, mood, relatedness, affect, use of environment, thematic development, and your own subjective feelings—your judgment about the particular child is made by comparing his or her functioning with the age-appropriate styles and levels of functioning. In other words, after you have compiled detailed descriptions of the child's functioning in each category, ask yourself how this child's capacities compare with the age- and developmental stage-appropriate norms.

Table 1 in Chapter 3, which offers illustrative examples of developmental phase- and age-appropriate levels of functioning for each category, will help orient you to these standards. Their usefulness lies in guiding you in the development of your own internal chart so that awareness of these expectations will reside at an intuitive as well as at a cognitive level. The internal chart takes form gradually as you gain experience with scores of clinical interviews. Then you literally feel something amiss when you deal with a child who is not functioning at age-appropriate levels, and this intuitive sense is the clue that prompts a search for what, specifically, the child is doing or saying (or not doing or saying) that falls short of expectations.

A special word about *content* is in order here. Judgments about the content of a child's themes, in contradistinction to those about thematic structural elements such as organization and sequence, should be held in abeyance until you have fully understood the unique circumstances of the child's life. With regard to issues of content, knowledge of the familial, societal, and cultural factors at work will contribute importantly to your interpretation. Thus, you may notice that a child's content seems idiosyncratic and out of sync with what is usually seen at this phase and age. In order to judge whether this child's concerns reflect an extraordinarily adaptive coping strategy, a reasonable manner of coping, or a pathological style, you must first become knowledgeable about the family circumstances and the historical perspective that engendered these concerns. As your experience broadens and deepens, your sense of age-appropriate concerns in varying contexts will sharpen correspondingly and surprises will occur less often.

With respect to those categories that reflect process and structure—e.g., thematic organization, organization of affects, and relatedness (or nonrelatedness)—the experienced clinician finds that the questions and tentative hypotheses generated by the interview hold up fairly well when examined in the light of information from other sources. In these categories, one's direct observations in what is admittedly only a cross-sectional setting (the clinical interview) regularly show a satisfying consistency with other data.

Let us say that your internal chart of developmental phase- and age-appropriate levels of functioning is reasonably well developed and you have

131

justifiable confidence in your abilities to observe a child in the interview in all the senses we have previously discussed. At this point I would suggest to you a framework for forming hypotheses regarding a child's developmental status based on the interview data alone. The framework consists of a series of three basic questions and related subquestions. Using the observations made in each of the categories, you seek a determination, or hypothetical answer, to each question.

The first question in the series is: What is the level of the basic ego functions, including (a) the organic or neurophysiological components of ego functioning, and (b) the functional or psychological aspects of ego functioning, and how do these levels compare with the age-appropriate developmental levels?

To determine the level of functioning of the organic components of the ego you would examine such aspects as motor coordination, sensory systems, sensorimotor integration, cognition, and the capacity to concentrate and focus attention. Intelligence, a product of multiple factors, would be included in your determination, as would specific cognitive or learning difficulties insofar as they are based on the physical maturation of the central nervous system. Since intelligence and cognitive difficulties are rarely determined solely by "organic" factors, however, one must always consider the functional factors as well.

With regard to psychological aspects of ego functioning, compare the child's actual psychological capacities with the age-expected capacities for reality testing, impulse regulation, and mood organization, and stability; also compare the child's capacities to organize and refine a sense of self, to integrate and organize emotions, and to think.

Certain categories are obviously pertinent to the task of assessing ego functions. Data from the second category, relatedness, will help to determine the age-appropriateness of the child's capacity for forming human relationships as well as his or her capacity to delineate a sense of self. Data from the third category, mood, will help to determine if the child is below the age-appropriate level in the capacity to organize and stabilize mood. Your descriptive data in the fourth category will yield clues to whether the basic structure of the child's personality in terms of organizing emotions and integrating them with thought is at the appropriate age level. With regard to the way the child deals with anxiety, look for grossly disorganizing anxiety that is inconsistent with age expectations. For example, we would not be surprised at disorganizing anxiety in a 3-year-old, but would be concerned if the same degree of disorganization appeared after an anxious interaction with a 7- or 8-year-old.

In looking at the thematic category, we would not be as concerned with thematic sequence as with the capacity for age- and phase-appropriate thematic organization. Does an 8-year-old seemingly bring themes "out of left field," as illustrated in Chapter 2 by the child who talked about his body falling apart without any buildup or link to earlier themes, thereby demonstrating a possible difficulty in distinguishing fantasy from reality and/or the beginning of a "thought disorder"? With regard to one's own subjective impressions, at times one will get an uncanny sense of something most unusual about a child, which may be a tip-off that his or her personality organization is not age-appropriate.

Once you have compared the child's level of functioning with the age-appropriate norms in our observational categories, you should ask yourself about the "autonomous" ego functions; namely, creativity, curiosity, and intellectual capacity. You want to know if the child has strengths or weaknesses in these areas of ego functioning.

If you do nothing else in a diagnostic session, you want to make sure that you observe whether a child's basic ego functions are below the age-appropriate level. You do not want to overlook the fact that an 8-year-old with superficial learning problems is functioning psychologically at a 5- or 6-year-old level. Such oversights are frequently made with children because of the subtleties associated with the functioning appropriate to each particular age.

With very young children, for example, in whom you expect the distinction between reality and fantasy to be blurred, it is sometimes difficult to determine whether or not a child is at an age-appropriate level. A 3½-year-old who shows you no evidence of realistic interaction with the environment may be manifesting less than age-appropriate functioning along the lines of differentiating self from nonself. On the other hand, if you notice this lag intermittently in some areas and not in others, you may be witnessing a normal developmental performance. A 4- or 5-year-old child may say he is scared because there is a monster who comes in at night, hides under his bed, and keeps him from sleeping. When you ask if that is a dream, the child says, "No, that's a real monster. I'm afraid to look under my bed." At these early ages the capacity for fantasy is often quite robust. Yet many children, if you press them by saying, "Come on, it's make-believe even though I know it feels real," will admit that you have put it correctly. They can make

133

the distinction when you press them. On the other hand, you may see children who are unable to make the distinction. In many such cases further inquiry may reveal that their problem in this area is narrowly circumscribed, the boundary between primary- and secondary-process thinking being impaired only in regard to certain kinds of fearful fantasies; you may even uncover structured phobias.

In general, you have to make very subtle distinctions in assessing the basic ego functions of children aged 3 to 6, for these are the years when such ego functions are actually developing. Your picture of whether basic functions—such as differentiation of and self from nonself, as well as the capacity to test reality—are below expectations depends largely on issues of context and pervasiveness. If a blur between fantasy and reality occurs in one limited context—for instance, at night, when even adults hearing a noise will think there is an intruder in the house—you would not think of a lag in reality testing. If, however, a 4-year-old thinks "crooks are following me" all day long, you may consider the possibility that there is a distortion in certain age-appropriate ego functions.

Although the difficulty of assessing basic ego functions is greater when you are observing younger children, and thus sometimes the source of inappropriate diagnoses, older children can also be hard to assess. For example, there are latency-age children with organized delusional systems who keep their problems fairly secret. They may give you one or two clues in the playroom—a bizarre stare or a weird giggle—but on the whole behave in a reasonably appropriate manner, causing you to miss their inability to differentiate fantasy from reality.

It may be especially hard to assess basic ego functioning in troubled teenagers. You may see teenagers with multiple symptoms of depression and anxiety and, with so much to assess in terms of symptoms, simply fail to observe more severe psychopathology, such as a basic deficit in ego functioning. Such misses are exceedingly unfortunate because often, if the treatment program is not aimed at the most fundamental problem, a child capable of full recovery and growth is unable to realize it.

For instance, take the case of a young woman with multiple phobias who was seeing a hypnotherapist. Beginning in adolescence, the girl had seen four or five psychiatrists who had focused in various ways on her "neurotic" symptoms. She had always functioned superficially well and had the kind of symptoms that could easily be viewed as neurotic. No one ever saw that there was an underlying difficulty in organizing themes and rich, age-appropriate affects. In other words, there was a subtle thought disorder. By the time she was seeing the hypnotherapist, she had deteriorated to the point of being unable to work or live on her own. Whether this deterioration could have been prevented cannot be determined; yet, from the material presented it appeared that there would have been a good chance of improvement rather than deterioration if her core vulnerability in basic ego functions—rather than merely the more superficial symptoms—had been treated.

In addition to looking for obvious departures from age-appropriate norms of ego functioning—i.e., delusions, hallucinations, loosening of associations in the sense we have talked about, wildly inappropriate affects—it is important to be attuned to the subtler departures: those that give you a sense of a hazy boundary between the self and the nonself. This haziness arises from disordered development in the period from ages 2 to 4, when the capacity for symbol-making begins to emerge and the developmental task of differentiating self from other at a symbolic level, is achieved (see Mahler's [1975] description of the individuation process).

Some people never quite master the differentiation of self from other at the level of mental representation. Such people will temporarily manifest less than age-appropriate reality testing, affect modulation, and integration of thought and affect, and then quickly recover appropriate age-level behavior. Basically, they suffer an impairment in the capacity to differentiate fully all experiences which are related to the self from all those related to the nonself. To spot such an impairment in the children you interview, look into the categories covering emotional tone and relatedness; particularly examine the child's capacity to organize themes and communication patterns, and be aware of your own subjective feelings.

By conceptualizing the child's functioning in a developmental framework (i.e., comparing the child's functioning levels with age-appropriate levels) one gains a precision of identification not readily available in the pathological descriptive framework. Thus, rather than having a global diagnosis to work with (e.g., the child is psychotic), it is more helpful to a therapist's treatment program to have the specific ego impairments spelled out (e.g., the capacity for thematic organization in this 6-year-old is at the level of a 3-year-old). Identification of the child's problem in a developmental context allows the therapist to see more clearly the degree and area of impairment. I will have more to say later about the advantages of the developmental approach to diagnosis.

135

Assuming that you have ascertained that the personality organization (basic ego functioning) is intact, the second question in the series is: What is the degree of ego rigidity in relation to age-appropriate rigidity? Or conversely, is this child capable of phase- and age-appropriate flexibility? Can this child experience the ranges of feelings, thoughts, and interpersonal relationship patterns appropriate to his or her age and developmental phase? Can the child employ the appropriate adaptive, coping, and defensive maneuvers?

Certain children are able to maintain intact personality functioning (reality testing, impulse regulation, mood stabilization, and overall affect organization) only at the expense of relinquishing age- and phase-expected flexibility. Such children may forgo genuine contact with others, for example; their relationships are shallow, mechanical, devoid of the warmth of human intimacy. Others may give up assertiveness or aggressiveness; they are passive, compliant, and mildly withdrawn. In such children we see a "walling off" of certain areas of human experience—pleasure and intimacy in the former; assertiveness and mastery in the latter—in the service of maintaining their capacity for intact personality functioning. These are children who are operating on a narrow stage and playing out but one drama. All their affects are colored by this one drama. They have constricted their range of experiences.

For example, you may interview a child who cannot tolerate any experience of human feelings. He tends to live in an impersonal and concrete experiential world where he relates mainly to inanimate objects. Although such a child might come in and talk to you in a seemingly normal way, you sense his impersonal level of attachment. The child might focus on inanimate objects in the room, show considerable interest in how things work, and be quite organized and logical in approaching the inanimate world, but a spark would be missing; such a child lacks a range of affects and allows no meaningful affective involvement with you or with friends, parents, or siblings. He may talk about building an airplane with friends, but you get no sense either of pleasure or competitive aggressiveness. This boy, early in life and perhaps with good reason, may have made a pivotal, though not intentional, decision; perhaps one could say his developmental processes made a decision for him. He may have decided that in order to protect his basic ego functions, in order to remain in this world and not go "crazy," he has to limit himself to a range of experience that excludes human feelings.

136

Other examples of constriction include children who, for fear of losing mother's love, may give up any awareness of angry feelings, and experience only sadness and depression. In other words, they are frightened because they were never able to work out that they could get angry at mother—that she would not abandon them as a result. Their basic ego development has occurred, therefore their basic reality testing is intact. Their object constancy is solidified enough for them to proceed to the Oedipal phase. Because they are frightened of the conscious experience of anger and of the behavioral experience of assertiveness, however, the whole area of anger and assertiveness is cut off.

Often children with some degree of ego rigidity do not have problems until much later in their lives when one or another developmental demand puts them under stress. An illustration would be the person who had peer relationships on a fairly concrete level as a child but felt extremely uncomfortable when it came time to date and have more intimate relationships. Only then, in adolescence, did he begin to feel isolated and to experience depression. On reflection, you would be able to see a pattern stemming from childhood in which certain kinds of pleasurable and affectionate yearnings were walled off.

Another example would be the child who throughout her early development demonstrated a strong and assertive character. As she matured, she took over many leadership roles and was considered a healthy, model teenager. Yet, as she entered her twenties and separated from her family, she became quite depressed and withdrawn. What had been overlooked in her youth was her inability to deal with passivity and its associated longings. Early in life she had walled off affects and themes related to passivity. A playroom session with such a person at the age of 8 might have revealed an absence of empathy, dependent yearnings, an inability to cope with loss and to experience sadness, and an overinvestment in assertive and aggressive themes. If the situation had been reversed, that is, if she had been a passive, preoccupied child who was not doing well in school, she might well have come to the attention of a teacher and received any necessary treatment.

As indicated, both intuitive awareness and cognitive knowledge of age-appropriate proclivities are crucial for assessing ego rigidity. Use the information from the descriptive categories to make this assessment of a specific child. In the category of relatedness (again, assuming you have already determined that there is a capacity for relatedness), look at the style and range in terms of the age expectations. Does this 5-year-old—who ought to be capable of a rich, wide-ranging emotional style—actually have a shallow and constricted style? Is this 8-year-old—who should be capable of some empathy, sharing, and mutual regard—clinging and demanding? In the category of mood, is there a fixed stereotypical mood inconsistent with age-appropriate capacities? Is the 5-year-old—who ought to be expansive and joyous—sad, depressed, and sober-looking during the entire interview? Is the range of affect in an 8-year-old limited to competitive strivings with games of shooting and one person beating up another, or is there a range of affects reflecting competitiveness, lovingness, protectiveness, orderliness? In the category of thematic development, look at the richness and depth of themes elaborated. Are certain age-appropriate themes absent? For instance, take the case of a 5-year-old who is not developing intricate family dramas involving competition, rivalry, intrigue, and curiosity but instead is playing out only one drama reflecting emotional hunger and the fear of being hurt. The richness and depth of the themes clue you to those areas that are being experienced and those that are not.

The child's affects, thoughts, and interpersonal experience—to the extent that they are revealed in the interview—give you a detailed picture of the relative richness or poverty of the child's inner life, which you can then compare with the expected norm. Moreover, they give you a sense of what it feels like inside the child's skin. For example, a child may not have any overt problems, but the shallowness of his inner life is conveyed by the few primitive affects he manifests. You observe only some sadness, a little envy, a little jealousy: you see no capacity for love, empathy, or sharing; no competitiveness or assertiveness; you sense the child's inner emptiness. You see him play with peers, but in shallow ways. Your notes show that the thematic content in the playroom failed to develop; that your own customary interest, curiosity, and personal warmth failed to materialize. In sum, even though there were no major symptoms in evidence—in fact, it was not even clear why the child was brought in—you have both observed and sensed that he has little depth. What is missing can be assumed to be walled off or rigidified. Something in this child's personality is not being differentiated, integrated, and synthesized.

The concept of rigidity is relative rather than absolute. I like to use the analogy of a balloon to describe this range of internal human experiences. The balloon is fully and evenly inflated in children who are functioning at the age-appropriate level in all facets of the observational categories. In children whose functioning is impaired in a circumscribed area (e.g., a structured phobia), a weak spot or bruise is visible in one area of the balloon, but the balloon is flexible and can stretch to maintain its symmetry. The look of the balloon that represents children with more extensive impairment would be lopsided; some sections are stretched tight while others are limp and collapsed. Such children would be functioning to some degree—able to attend school, for example, and to carry out adequate reality testing—but they have developed pervasive character distortions such as obsessive-compulsive or hysterical patterns. To complete the analogy, balloons of such poor quality material that they burst at the slightest provocation represent children with the most flagrantly impaired basic ego functioning. These children would be spotted by means of the first question in the series. Unlike children with some degree of flexibility in basic ego functioning, such deeply troubled children are incapable of encapsulating their problems or narrowing their range of experience to protect themselves. Rather, they often exacerbate their difficulties because their reality testing is totally inadequate. Thus, a child hampered by some age-inappropriate rigidity, finding himself in over his head, will swim back to shore and sit on the beach; but a child whose basic ego functioning is age-inappropriate will, in similar circumstances, swim farther out and deny, often grandiosely, that there is any trouble at all.

To illustrate the difference between a less-than-flexible balloon and one of the poorest quality, let us say you are observing an 8-year-old girl who is facing a stressful situation; you ask yourself, What is her range of coping strategies? For instance, if she has only mild rigidity, she might use a little denial, some reaction formation or projection, or, more sophisticatedly, she might show some capacity for sublimatory channels. With moderate rigidity, she instead would become somewhat irritable, as well as a little negativistic or argumentative, but would remain continually involved with family and friends. A severe impairment would be indicated if she suffered a major regression and withdrew from human relationships; began behaving negativistically and impulsively; began to lose control of urine and feces.

Let us now look at the kinds of behavior that characterize various degrees of rigidity in the functioning of basic ego structures which are fundamentally intact. At the level of serious impairment (the lopsided balloon), you might see paranoia, mild schizoid patterns, or passive-aggressive patterns as a basic way of life. If such behavior patterns are not present, you want to see if only a small part of the balloon is cut off, which would represent a relatively moderate walling off of experience.

An example would be the child who evinces pleasure; who is sweet and somewhat passive; whose range of affects shows no assertiveness, aggression, or competition, but does show all the other age-appropriate affects; and whose thematic content matches the affect—that is, it shows no competitiveness, envy, jealousy, assertiveness, or fighting. Although the child's mood and the basic relatedness to you are appropriate, certain age-appropriate components do not emerge in the course of the interview. Such a configuration of observations is consistent with a child whose flexibility is not at the appropriate age level. Such a child is more psychologically developed than a schizoid child who gives up all affective involvement, for the former gives up only the affects that scare him or her. The former child has not experienced a major "shutdown," or cutting off of experience, early in life, but instead has experienced certain affects as frightening and has therefore decided to give them up. The fact that the child has had some involvement—albeit brief—with the now missing pieces of his experiential world will make your therapeutic task easier.

The mildest manifestation of rigidity (an abscess in the balloon) could be termed an encapsulated limitation. Here, the overall ego structure is basically flexible in all of the categories mentioned. By and large, the child is able to engage the world in an age-appropriate manner. That is to say, the child's neurophysiology, human relationships, mood, range of affects and stability of affects under stress, and thematic organization (particularly the sequence of themes) are all age-appropriate. However, there is a contextually significant area that is walled off; often you will find it to be closely associated with any symptoms that the child may be suffering. In certain areas where there are conflicts, neurotic mechanisms work to encircle the conflicts and keep them from spreading, and thus protect the child from regressing characterologically. Using our analogy of a theater stage, the stage of a child with encapsulated limitations is the appropriate size, and sound enough to contain wide-ranging dramas that have both age-appropriate themes and themes from earlier phases of development. But you notice some bumps and snags in the flooring, which the child has to avoid as he or she performs the drama.

An encapsulated disorder—e.g., a phobia such as fear of elevators—protects the flexibility of the rest of the personality in the same way an abscess protects the rest of the body from infection. Let us say that a child is referred to you because of marked symptoms of a phobic nature. The child is doing well in school and enjoying good peer relationships; he develops themes around competition, aggression, and envy as well as compassion, empathy, loving, and caring. You feel he has handled his range of concerns in an organized way. But as you look closely at the thematic sequence, which is where you get your clues to what is going on with such a child, you see that, in addition to the symptoms of nightmares, phobia, or mild sibling rivalry, there are related problems. You observe an undue amount of anxiety around certain themes. For instance, there is a sudden disruption when the subject of competition with siblings arises. In response to your comment, "I know kids have a lot of different feelings about brothers and sisters," the child, instead of opening up this area, shows some constriction. He says, "Oh, yes. Of course, most kids love their brothers and sisters and they ought to," and continues to talk about the protective, loving dimensions of having siblings while strictly avoiding competitive, angry thoughts. Even more commonly, a child with a flexible ego structure who has some Oedipal conflicts may talk a lot about the competition and anger but say nothing about his curiosity concerning the more pleasurable interests that arise in the context of the family drama. Such interests have been walled off. As you move in on this and say, "You know, kids usually have a lot of curiosity and interest about what goes on with their parents," the child says, "Oh no, not me," or "That doesn't happen," or "I don't know what you are talking about," suddenly becoming naive and acting "dumb" when you touch on this anxiety-laden theme. Here you see a walling off of the experiential world in a contextually narrow range and area, often dynamically defined. If you were to ask a healthy Oedipal child the same question, he might talk about how he tried to break into the parents' bedroom, or how he went into the bathroom with his father.

An encapsulated limitation in flexibility such as a phobia or an obsessive ritual might seem more serious than a moderate but pervasive constriction because the former is more obvious. A phobia or obsessive ritual can be seen as a developmental accomplishment, however, in the sense that the capacity for neurosis implies a high level of integration in a rather flexible ego structure. Nagera (1966) has discussed the notion that the infantile neurosis, which forms the foundation for later neurotic conflicts, reflects a substantial developmental achievement. That is, a child cannot be neurotic until he or she has achieved an Oedipal—and therefore rather advanced—level of development. Thus, a neurotic disorder in itself implies that development has proceeded well in terms of personality flexibility.

It should be emphasized, however, that an encapsulated limitation is one which successfully protects the personality's flexibility. If the symptom in question does interfere with going to school, having friends, or enjoying the full range of pleasurable and assertive affects and themes, then we are not dealing with an encapsulated limitation, which we have defined as one that protects the personality. The behavior of a child with an encapsulated limitation is not seriously below the appropriate age level. Of course, neurotic conflicts can and do occur in the presence of other, more pervasive impairments. You must make your diagnosis systematically. If the child's developmental level in certain ego functions is significantly below normal, that is your primary diagnosis. You must patch up the cracks in the stage before you can work on the dynamics of a particular neurotic conflict.

Each level of inflexibility (constriction) may be further delineated in terms of specific subtypes. In other words, a limitation in the flexibility of the balloon can take many different forms, which are discussed below.

## Major Constrictions

The integrity of basic personality functioning may be maintained at the price of flexibility in the overall character structure. Massive avoidance of dangerous areas of life experience, or massive inhibition of wishes, thoughts, or affects, allows the child to stay away from situations that will cause a breakdown of ego functions (e.g., severe schizoid or paranoid characters, negativistic personalities, severe depressive characters, or narcissistic disorders).

Children with such a constricted adjustment do not normally show signs of ego defects. They function adequately—within the constrictions of their characters—without special vulnerability to fragmentation. The price they pay is a serious restriction of their life experiences. Such a child may live a relatively symptom-free life by avoiding stressful experiences. For example, a child with a limitation in the capacity to modulate affect might use avoidance to stay away from feeling states that are perceived as dangerous. In the clinical interview one might notice a highly idiosyncratic or *very* restricted thematic and affective range as well as style of relatedness. Specific subtypes of constrictions and impairments in flexibility are outlined below.

One major constriction is *limitation of experience of feelings and/or thoughts.* For example, a child does not experience warm, loving feelings and avoids intimate one-to-one relationships (e.g., the schizoid type of personality). He may appear distant and aloof in interviews, remaining on an emotionally flat level in spite of significant time spent with the interviewer. Another child (e.g., one who is chronically depressed) restricts her internal affective experience; she does not permit herself angry or assertive feelings, but experiences only passive sadness. Behaviorally she is limited to apathetic, mildly withdrawn actions. Yet another child may not be able to tolerate dependent wishes, and will appear too self-reliant and somewhat unconcerned.

Another constriction is *alteration and limitation of pleasure orientation,* as, for example, manifested in the perversions. This loss of flexibility is often accompanied by a stereotyped, intense pleasure orientation limited to a few areas. That is, certain kinds of pleasure cannot be experienced. In the interview the style of relatedness, affects, and thematic sequence may have a persistent tone centering on one theme, such as sadistic pleasure or a particular body part, without any signs of compassionate, warm, empathic pleasure. The behavior may also express sadistic themes and concerns with certain anatomical zones.

*Major externalization of internal events,* such as conflicts, feelings, and thoughts, is another character distortion. The child who externalizes hostile internal wishes or feelings may perceive aggression as persistently coming from the outside. Themes of "they are out to get me" may dominate the interview. Another, less severe syndrome of externalization is seen in those children who externalize perceptions about themselves (such as low self-esteem) onto others (e.g., saying in the interview, "I know you find me icky"); or those who act out their internal conflicts by polarizing their views, taking one side of the conflict themselves and provoking others to speak for the opposite side. For example, a child might externalize his self-criticism by acting in a way that provokes his parents to be critical of him; or in the interview, by provoking the clinician to manifest a critical attitude.

Another constriction is the *limitation of internalizations necessary for regulation of impulses, affects, and thoughts.* The person with an underlying difficulty in internal regulation does not see his impulsiveness as a symptom. It would, however, become apparent in the interviews; for example, when a theme of separation is immediately followed by a theme of impulsiveness or by impulsive behavior. In the process of the clinical interview such a youngster may demonstrate little patience, continually vacillating between self-gratification ("Where is the candy?") and impulsive behavior (e.g., breaking your furniture).

The child with a *limitation in self-esteem maintenance* manages to maintain a surprisingly stable personality superficially (albeit with intolerance for failure, and problems with empathy and intimacy). Such children may present a shallow quality of engagement while attempting to impress the interviewer with their own importance. In the interview, they may show little capacity for genuine warmth or empathy and, after a few interviews, will vacillate between relying on the interviewer for a sense of self-worth or self-esteem, and turning to unrealistic grandiose fantasies for such support. If the interviewer is able to engage such children, they may eventually communicate a deep sense of emptiness and vulnerability, with tremendous fear of loss. Such children are constricted in the capacity to experience self-worth, self-esteem, and a range of compassionate and empathic feelings toward others.

Persons with a mild *instability in self-object differentiation* are vulnerable to a limited breakdown of that capacity, followed by reorganization. For example, under stress these children may either lose some control over affect or impulses, or show a disorganization in their thematic sequence. Their lives are not generally unstable because they restrict their experiences to avoid stress, but they can regress toward dedifferentiation. Such children may, therefore, when pressed in an interview, present mild fragmentation in their communication patterns.

## Moderate Character or Personality Constrictions

Disorders consisting of moderate character constrictions (e.g., moderate obsessive-compulsive or hysterical personality patterns, some limited impulsive behavior, a tendency toward externalization) involve the same categories of inflexibility of personality (characterological constriction) as above, but to a lesser degree. Only certain aspects of the personality evidence chronic repetitive limitations—in contrast to constriction of the entire personality in severer disorders.

## Encapsulated Disorders

Encapsulated disorders protect the flexibility of the personality by producing limited impairments related to symptoms and contextually specific character traits. They differ from characterological constrictions in a very important way; that is, they do not involve avoidance of broad areas of experience. Encapsulated disorders also do *not* involve chronic, repetitive avoidance or limitations of thoughts, wishes, and affects. For example, whereas anger in general is avoided in a character constriction, in an encapsulated disorder only anger directed at a *contextually significant* other might be avoided (e.g., anger at an authority figure associated with one's father). Similarly, a pleasurable feeling will be avoided only in contextually relevant situations. While these feelings are usually identified by dynamic hypotheses, they are also directly observable.

## Encapsulated Symptom Disorders

The major limitations and alterations seen in symptom encapsulations are in thought and affect. The first type, *limitation of thought,* is found, for example, in "hysterical" symptoms such as periodic dizziness. Aside from such symptoms the child may function at an age-appropriate level: engage in warm, loving relationships; be assertive; and experience empathy and concern as well as anger and aggression. Only a narrow content area of psychic life dealing with specific wishes (e.g., of a pleasurable nature) is walled off. In the interview, the limitation of thought may become apparent only by the continued absence of this specific content in an otherwise flexible child who evinces a wide range of themes.

The second major type of symptom-encapsulated disorder is *limitation or alteration of affect* (e.g., as seen in obsessive or compulsive patterns). In the interview such children may evince the absence of specific affects in certain contextual situations (e.g., they may not evince anger at the interviewer when such a response would be expected, and/or be unable to evidence thematic trends dealing with anger toward certain contextually significant figures).

Encapsulated disorders are usually not difficult to diagnose. The child shows a broad range of age-appropriate themes and affects, and a reasonable interpersonal engagement with the interviewer. However, in certain contextually evident areas he is capable of only limited affective range and/or thematic depth. There is an obvious disparity between the otherwise flexible personality and the encapsulated areas.

## Encapsulated Character Limitations

These disorders present themselves not so much in specific symptoms (phobias, compulsive rituals, or conversion reactions), but rather as subtle limitations in the flexibility of the personality. These disorders differ from the earlier, severer constrictions of personality both in the narrowness of the area that is limited and in the mildness of the symptoms, if there are any. These disorders are related both to contextually relevant thoughts and affects (e.g., problems with certain types of peers or teachers) and to stress.

They differ from the symptom disorders in that they are not as narrowly focused and often not as intense. An issue may express itself in these disorders in a more diffuse way through a large number of behaviors or thematic expressions. For example, a child with an encapsulated compulsive symptom may repetitively wash her hands; in contrast, a child with an obsessional encapsulated character limitation might be too thorough in his attitude toward school and "getting things completed," may have difficulties expressing his feelings, and may be too self-critical.

A phobic encapsulated symptom (e.g., a fear of height) would be fixed and relatively intense. On the other hand, a phobic encapsulated *character disorder* would probably include phobic attitudes of a milder nature (e.g., a child who is generally fearful and tends to use avoidance a great deal).

In general, neurotic encapsulated character formations may be categorized along the same lines as the severer character constrictions (with the understanding that the encapsulated disorders are less intense and are related to specific contextually significant experiences rather than to pervasive domains of experience). Thus an *encapsulated limitation of feeling or thought* in a major life area is represented in the child who invariably shies away from the slightest emotional confrontation with authority figures, but whose other areas of emotional experience are not constricted. An *encapsulated alteration in pleasure orientation* might be shown by the child who has difficulty enjoying certain (but not all) types of age-appropriate pleasurable play. An *encapsulated externalization of internal conflict* is seen in the child who blames others for her own behavior in contextually relevant areas. An *encapsulated impairment in self-esteem regulation* is seen in the otherwise emotionally healthy child who easily becomes morose when he loses a game with a contextually significant peer or adult.

### Transient Developmental Conflicts and Stresses

To continue the balloon analogy, children with perfectly inflated balloons are fully engaged in a flexible way in phase-appropriate experiences (intrapsychic, interpersonal, etc.). Nevertheless, such children may have transient developmental conflicts; e.g., the child who has nightmares while working through the final stages of the Oedipal phase of development. In addition, one might also observe situational reactions, such as transient anxiety or depression in response to a family crisis. The point is that a healthy, happy child fully involved in age- and phase-appropriate experiences may yet suffer considerable transient discomfort and even symptomatic behavior in the service of developmental progress and adaptive coping with environmental or intrapsychic stress.

Our first two questions—what is the level of basic ego functions, and what is the degree of ego rigidity—tell us about the stage on which the drama is being played, or, in other words, about the structure of the personality. We want to know whether this stage is constructed to meet the age-appropriate standards of integrity and flexibility. If the integrity or flexibility is below expectation, we want to know what parts of the stage are affected and to what degree. If the child is functioning only slightly below age expectations, such a lag might reflect a somewhat slow maturation or the interference of environmental circumstances. But what if the child is clearly one or two major developmental steps behind his age-appropriate level of accomplishment?

Clinical judgments begin to emerge as we compare our observations of the child's functioning with the age-appropriate level. If we have observed that the basic ego functioning is two or three developmental steps below the age-appropriate level—which raises serious questions about the integrity of the personality—then there is a need for further documentation, and the prospect of intensive treatment is considered. Or we may have a child whose basic ego functions are at the age-appropriate level but whose flexibility of personality structure is below expectations by two or three developmental steps. We see that major areas of age-appropriate life experience—such as the capacity for pleasure with peers or the mastery of school requirements —are walled off. In such cases, different considerations regarding treatment recommendations will be required. Another child may show age-inappropriate rigidity in a few confined areas of functioning but otherwise function at age level, indicating many strengths in his personality structure. One sort of treatment recommendation would be made if we judged the disorder to be an encapsulated limitation. If, however, we judge that the area of rigidity is a full developmental level behind age expectations and, moreover, seems fixed there (i.e., if we find no reason to assume that the rigidity is a response to chronic or acute environmental stress), then we would consider different, perhaps more intensive, treatment recommendations aimed at helping the child attain the expected age level in all sectors of development.

This brings us to the third and last question in the series: What are the particular concerns of the child? We look at these concerns in relation to what brought the child in for consultation and in the context of the overall personality structure. In other words, we cannot adequately consider the drama without knowing all about the stage. The drama of aggression, rivalry, and retaliation plays very differently if enacted on a stage which has great holes and cracks versus a stage which is broad, strong, and sturdy. The soundly built stage can well accommodate an intense drama; the poorly made one might very well cave in under the action. All too often, those conducting clinical interviews erroneously zoom in on this third question —the concerns and conflicts—before they make their hypotheses about the integrity of the overall personality structure and its relative flexibility or rigidity.

The child's concerns can be examined from the point of view of their organization, nature, and age appropriateness. The observational categories are helpful to this task. Within the categories, focus more on content than you have done heretofore. Look at the content of the style of relatedness; the particular content and dimensions of the child's mood; the content and sequence of the child's specific predominant affects. Look at the sequence of themes that the child expresses during the interview. Match up the way the child shifts both his relatedness to you and his affects with the sequence of his themes; this matching will help you sketch out the child's particular drama and concerns. As an example, recall the child discussed in Chapter 2, who came in with themes about shooting, shifted to the theme of protecting his brother, and then expressed curiosity about his parents and about his own body. The range of his affects and moods coupled with his specific thematic sequence gave us a picture of some of his particular concerns.

The following outline provides a summary of the categories that are important in determining answers to each of the three questions.

### Observational Categories for Constructing a Developmental Diagnostic Formulation

1. The level of basic ego functions
   a. Organic functioning
      (1) Physical and neurological development
   b. Psychological functioning
      (1) Capacity for relatedness
      (2) Capacity for organizing mood

(3) Capacity for affects and anxieties
(4) Capacity for organizing themes
(5) Subjective reaction of interviewer

2. The degree of personality rigidity
   a. Style and range of relatedness
   b. Stereotypical mood
   c. Range of affect
   d. Richness and depth of themes
   e. Subjective reaction of interviewer

3. The child's concerns and conflicts
   a. Content and style of relatedness
   b. Content of mood
   c. Content and sequence of specific affects
   d. Sequence of themes

This chapter has focused on what I have called the developmental approach to diagnosis, and little has been said about the implications for treatment recommendations per se. While treatment will not be considered in this work, a few brief illustrative comments about treatment may be useful and may suggest areas for further discussion. For example, where there are serious developmental lags in basic personality functions (e.g., reality testing, impulse regulations), an intensive program integrating structured supports such as a therapeutic day program or school and supportive, dynamically oriented psychotherapy is indicated. As treatment progresses, the supportive and structured features of treatment may in balance give way to a more in-depth approach.

Where there are major rigidities in important sectors of experience (e.g., a child who is one or two developmental stages behind), an intensive, long-term, dynamically oriented psychotherapeutic approach is indicated. The child with more circumscribed but chronic and intense difficulties (e.g., around assertive and aggressive feelings, or around intimate feelings) may also benefit from an intensive approach. In such cases one might expect positive, far-reaching results in a shorter time than with the more major rigidities. In some such cases, where there is a circumscribed difficulty of short duration, short-term dynamically oriented consultations or simply advice to parents, teachers, and others in the child's environment may be enough to help him work out his difficulty.

Finally, where we see a child who is basically at age level in the integrity of basic personality functions and overall flexibility but who is playing out a drama involving conflict, anxiety, and/or depression and is suffering some personal distress, we might consider different approaches. When the distressed child is the most available member of the family, short-term dynamic treatment may be extremely helpful. Where situational circumstances (e.g., a family conflict or school conflict) are contributing, some work with the environment might be indicated. It should be highlighted that work with the environment—family, parents, school, etc.—is usually indicated for all levels of impairment when it is thought that the environment may be harnessed to facilitate development. Furthermore, remedial education and physical-neurological approaches must also be considered where there are even questions of severe lags in central nervous system maturation and/or learning capacities.

A thorough diagnostic workup not only contributes to the overall treatment recommendation but also orients the clinician to the major issues that may need to be taken up in treatment: correcting defects, increasing age-appropriate flexibility, facilitating resolution of age-appropriate conflicts or stresses, etc. While the clinician is always alert to the patient's conflicts, the level and flexibility of ego structure guide his approach.

In this chapter I have tried to show how a particular clinical interview approach lends itself to the formulation of diagnostic hypotheses and preliminary judgments based on developmental considerations. A few comments should be made about the relationship of this approach to the traditional DSM-III psychiatric approach to children. As we have seen, the clinical judgments that can be deduced from the interviewing approach advanced here refer to the integrity or developmental level of basic ego functioning and flexibility, and the nature of the child's concerns or conflicts. These judgments parallel the traditional categories of psychiatric disability: psychosis (age-inappropriate level of basic ego functioning); character disorders (major limitations in flexibility in critical sectors of the personality); neurotic disturbances (encapsulated limitations in flexibility around certain areas of experience); and developmental conflicts (the difficulties experienced by the child with the "perfectly inflated balloon" as he or she works through particular developmental tasks).

In addition, a variety of learning and behavioral disorders based on neurological and/or physiological malfunction can be understood in the context of our approach to specific ego functions. These types of disorders, however, are also connected with the psychological aspects of ego functioning. For example, less than full attainment of an expected developmental level may show itself in a global impairment in the capacity to focus concentration; very circumscribed defect in an ego function, however, may result in only a mild impairment in the same capacity.

Considering the current preference for phenomenology, in contrast to what have been termed "inferred" dynamic states, it is also of interest that our diagnostic approach, although based on dynamic concepts, does not require "a belief" in internal states. Even when referring to children with encapsulated neurotic disorders—those who cannot process experience in a specified narrow domain—you can document the diagnosis *phenomenologically* in your playroom or on psychological testing, just as you can document phenomenologically that a person has hallucinations and delusions. The former is simply a subtler observation requiring, as it were, the high-power lens of your microscope.

As noted, the clinical judgments that can be derived from our approach are easily translated into the traditional or classical psychiatric concepts. What is being emphasized here, however, is that there may be an advantage to using a developmental framework because its concepts are not limited in explanatory value; they do have implications for pathogenesis and treatment of disorders. The developmental approach suggested here has, in addition, implications for both level of adaptation and level of psychopathology or limitation. Moreover, it has the unique virtue of enabling the interviewer to intuit the way a child experiences his own strengths and weaknesses, and thus to plan appropriate psychotherapeutic approaches.

In practice, the developmental approach presented here may be used together with traditional diagnostic classification schemes. A three-column approach may be used, with diagnoses based on symptoms and personality traits in one column; etiologically based diagnoses in another; and the developmental approach to diagnosis in still another. The developmental approach as described here suggests how the person "organizes" his experience and is in a sense the connection or "experiential pathway" between etiological circumstances and various manifest symptoms. See Table 2 for a summary of the developmental categories using the three-column approach. Note that symptom-oriented and etiologically based diagnoses are listed only for illustrative purposes and do not represent the full range of disorders that would correspond to each developmental impairment.

**Table 2** *A Developmental Approach to Diagnosis*

| ILLUSTRATIVE ETIOLOGICALLY BASED DIAGNOSES | DIAGNOSTIC CATEGORIES FROM A DEVELOPMENTAL APPROACH | ILLUSTRATIVE DIAGNOSES BASED ON SYMPTOMS AND PERSONALITY TRAITS (TRADITIONAL DSM-III, AXES I & II) |
|---|---|---|
| | 1. Significantly below age-appropriate level of ego functioning (ego defects) | |
| Infectious encephalopathy. Substance-induced organic mental disorders | a. Basic physical organic integrity of mental apparatus (perception, integration, motor, memory, regulation, judgment, etc.) | Mental retardation<br>Attentional deficit<br>Specific developmental disorders |
| | b. Structural psychological defects | Pervasive developmental disorder |
| | (1) Thought, reality testing, and organization | Childhood schizophrenia |
| | (2) Perception and regulation of affects | Affective disorders |
| | (3) Integration of affect and thought | |
| | (4) Defect in integration and organization, and/or in differentiation of self- and object representations | Borderline syndromes |
| | 2. Severe constrictions and alterations in age-appropriate level of ego structure | Behavior disorders<br>Conduct disorders<br>Personality disorders<br>Schizoid disorders |
| | a. Limitation of experience of feelings and/or thoughts in major life areas (love, learning, play) | |
| | b. Alterations and limitations in pleasure orientation | Psychosexual disorders |
| | c. Major externalizations of internal events (e.g., conflicts, feelings, thoughts) | Paranoid personality disorders |
| | d. Limitations in internalizations necessary for regulation of impulses, affect (mood), and thought | Impulse disorders |
| | e. Impairments in self-esteem regulation | Narcissistic disorders |

152

| ILLUSTRATIVE ETIOLOGICALLY BASED DIAGNOSES | DIAGNOSTIC CATEGORIES FROM A DEVELOPMENTAL APPROACH | ILLUSTRATIVE DIAGNOSES BASED ON SYMPTOMS AND PERSONALITY TRAITS (TRADITIONAL DSM-III, AXES I & II) |
|---|---|---|
| | f. Limited tendencies toward fragmentation of self-object differentiation | Dissociative disorders |
| | 3. Moderate constrictions and alterations in age-appropriate level of ego structure (same as above) | |
| | 4. Age-appropriate functioning, but with encapsulated disorders | |
| | a. Neurotic symptom formations | Anxiety disorders |
| | (1) Limitations and alterations in experience of areas of thought (hysterical repression); phobic displacements | Phobic disorders |
| | (2) Limitations and alterations in experience of affects and feelings (e.g., obsessional isolation—depressive turning of feelings against self) | Obsessive-compulsive disorders |
| | b. Age-appropriate level of functioning, but with neurotic encapsulated character formation | Mild forms of personality disorders |
| | (1) Encapsulated limitation of experience of feelings and thoughts in major life areas (love, work, play) | Mild obsessive-compulsive personality disorders |
| | (2) Encapsulated alterations and limitations in pleasure orientation | Mild psychosexual disorders |
| | (3) Encapsulated major externalizations of internal events (e.g., conflicts, feelings, thoughts) | Mild paranoid trends |

153

**Table 2** *A Developmental Approach to Diagnosis (Continued)*

| ILLUSTRATIVE ETIOLOGICALLY BASED DIAGNOSES | DIAGNOSTIC CATEGORIES FROM A DEVELOPMENTAL APPROACH | ILLUSTRATIVE DIAGNOSES BASED ON SYMPTOMS AND PERSONALITY TRAITS (TRADITIONAL DSM-III, AXES I & II) |
|---|---|---|
| | (4) Encapsulated limitations in internalizations necessary for regulation of impulses, affect (mood), and thought | Mild impulse disorders |
| | (5) Encapsulated impairments in self-esteem regulation | Mild narcissistic disorders |
| | 5. Basically age-appropriate, intact, flexible ego structures<br>   a. With phase-specific developmental conflicts | |
| |    b. With phase-specific, developmentally expected patterns of adaptation, including adaptive regressions | Adjustment disorders |
| |    c. Intact, flexible, developmentally appropriate ego structure | |

Note: All of the above structural alterations may have concomitant behavioral alterations, which will usually be described by the symptom cluster diagnoses.

In conclusion, it should be remembered that our discussion has concentrated on the clinical interview with the child and the resultant clinical judgments we can make about the child's functioning. We have not considered a number of the factors—earlier life experiences, current environmental stresses, family communication patterns, and a variety of other biological and environmental factors—that contribute so importantly to the child's functional status. Many would advocate that a full diagnostic system for children should delineate not only the child's manner of organizing his experiential world, which we are focusing on here, but also the dimensions and dynamics of the child's external world, particularly his family environment. I could not agree more with this position and again want to emphasize the limited applicability of this work, which focuses on the clinical interview with the child and is limited in scope to understanding how the child organizes his experiences in this situation.

The remainder of this chapter will focus on formulating hypotheses for the clinical interviews presented in Chapter 4, with the aim of illustrating the principles described above and providing important illustrative data on determining the child's concerns or conflicts.

### Formulations for Case 1

The basic organic components of Doug's ego appeared to be intact and at the age-appropriate level, as evidenced by his physical and neurological status (e.g., gross and fine motor coordination, speech, memory, level of intelligence). In contrast, although some basic ego functions were at the age-appropriate level, others were significantly below expectations. Thus, there was a capacity for intense relatedness but it had a hungry quality, indicating a degree of affect hunger more appropriate for a 2- or 3-year-old with some earlier deprivation. Similarly, mood was stable but overall had a depressed quality. The range of affect was not age-appropriate in that it was limited to concerns with illness, danger, robbers, and death. In addition, a quality of affect hunger predominated. On the other hand, Doug's organization and integration of affect and thought were at the age-appropriate level.

There was some indication of disruptive anxiety around the theme of his father's illness, and there was evidence of thought processes not in accord with a reality orientation when he talked about the "tape recorder" and his brother overhearing us. His thematic organization was therefore significantly below the age-appropriate level, reflecting *not* the organization of a late latency child but rather the occasional fragmentation (infusion of fantasy into reality) of a 3½- to 4½-year-old. Because Doug showed good capacity to recover a reality orientation, however, there is some question about the degree of the instability (under stress) of his reality orientation and capacity for thematic organization. On the whole, my observations raise a question about the integrity and age-appropriateness of basic ego functions.

While there is evidence of a subtle impairment in basic ego functioning, it should also be noted that for the most part this weakness is protected by a great deal of rigidity in his personality structure. The narrow range of his relatedness (hungry quality), his depressed mood, the narrow range of his affects, and his restricted thematic concerns all point to a rigid, vulnerable personality structure.

The nature of Doug's concerns—as evinced by the content of his relatedness and mood, and the sequence of his affects and themes—points to an unresolved preoccupation with early developmental issues of primitive envy (brother); fear of illness, injury, and death; and an inability to integrate (i.e., some ego splitting) the "robber" in him with his rigid ethical standards and desire to "protect" everyone. The use of projection around the theme of aggression and "being tape-recorded" indicates how disruptive his aggressive feelings are and how fragile are his defenses.

In sum, we have a primitive drama being played out on a very constricted stage with a subtle crack in it. Yet Doug also has a great deal of strength, as evinced by his capacity to relate, his desire for intimacy, his capacity to manifest anxiety and discomfort, and his intelligence.

## Formulations for Case 2

There is some question about the physical and organic aspects of Harold's basic ego functioning. His capacity for concentration seemed significantly below the age-appropriate level as he flitted around in a frenzied way from one activity to the next, at times quite careless about where he was throwing his ball. These activities seemed to be at a 3½- to 4-year-old level. While age is a key factor, temperamental differences might also dictate a child's activity level. Many 3½- and even some 2½-year-olds are capable of more focused concentration than this child. Nevertheless, by the time a child is 6 to 7½ one expects a more controlled capacity for focused concentration than Harold showed. In addition, problems with fine motor coordination and perceptual motor capacities, as exhibited by his overall drawing ability and his difficulty in making letters, indicate some significantly below age-appropriate functioning with respect to the maturation of his central nervous system.

In terms of the basic functional aspects of his ego, he seemed to be in accord with the reality of the playroom and was able to organize his affects and themes. At the same time, his behavior had a frantic, frenzied quality. He did not disorganize, however, and one theme followed the next in a seemingly logical manner. Moreover, affects and themes were integrated. Also, he did establish a sense of relatedness to me, though it was somewhat fugitive and not as involving as one would hope for a 7½-year-old.

While he came near to hitting me with the ball a few times, he did not show a gross impairment of age-expected impulse control; in addition, later in the interview he was able to respond to limits that I set when he was pulling at the strings of the drapes. Thus, although the basic ego functions were largely intact, he was below age-appropriate functioning in the quality and depth of his relatedness, and in his impulse control, which was not as well integrated as one would hope. With reference to the hypothesis raised above about the age-appropriateness of the organic component of his ego, it is reasonable to ask whether this possible impairment is interfering with and undermining his overall capacity to use his intact but slightly below age-appropriate ego functions.

Major limitations in the flexibility of his ego structure were observed. The sequences of his specific affects and themes pointed to his predominant concerns—aggression, power, winning and losing, being Superman and being fearful of attack. As we saw, there was little affective and thematic development of the empathic, loving, curious dimension of his personality; nor were his concerns with passivity and dependency elaborated. Such marked constrictions are representative of affects and concerns at the 3½- to 5-year-old level rather than the 7½-year-old level.

Constrictions were also noted in the style of his relatedness to me. He was not able to interact and communicate in a deep and rich manner, although he was able to relate superficially with constant eye contact. His relatedness to others may very well be compromised by the overall constriction noted above. That is, his concern with winning and losing—with having power and being attacked—dominates his personality at the expense of the capacities for exploration, warmth, empathy, and passive, dependent longings.

Therefore, we have a child struggling with his aggression and (possibly exaggerated) fear of being attacked. The stage on which he acts is constricted. It also has some fine cracks in those areas related to this boy's ability to modulate his concentration and his activity level as well as to coordinate and integrate his perceptions with his motor activity.

One might hypothesize that Harold is doing the best he can, given his inability to handle the driven quality of his activity level. Feeling driven, he organized himself around a "phallic aggressive mode," a developmental stage where his aggressive inclinations would be ascendant; however, he has been unable to go beyond this level of psychological development. The concerns he is playing out on his constricted and structurally compromised stage, therefore, seem to be overdetermined. There may be functional determinants as well as a maturational organic determinant.

When a child's behavior raises a number of hypotheses, especially ones concerning the organic aspects of ego structure (i.e., perceptual-motor capacities), we certainly want to get detailed psychological testing that focuses on these dimensions of ego functioning.

### Formulations for Case 3

Joan's basic organic integrity and basic ego functions were intact. She showed a rich style of relating and age-appropriate mood, range and organization of affects, and thematic organization and concerns (more or less).

With respect to the degree of age-appropriate flexibility of her personality, we would raise some questions. She needed help in getting started; initially she was silent. Although there was some range, her affects were predominantly focused on apprehensive and aggressive issues with hints of curiosity but little demonstration of warm curiosity, empathy, or love. Her thematic expression did develop some richness and depth but not an age-appropriate range; her concerns were focused on things falling off, people being poisoned and tricked, and the like. Mild fear, suspiciousness, teasing, and testing boundaries with her own aggression (e.g., wanting to throw the policeman doll out the window) dominated at the expense of seductiveness, curiosity, compassion, and early latency-level concerns. Therefore, the thematic sequence was more that of a 4½- to 5-year-old than of a 6-year-old.

Thus, we have a child whose age-appropriate ego structure has some limitations in flexibility. Her concerns with earlier-than-expected developmental issues are nevertheless within her current substage of development, although at the earlier end. Using our theatrical analogy, the stage is intact; it has appropriate width in some areas, is restricted in others, and is playing a drama slightly below age expectations but within Joan's overall developmental substage.

### Formulations for Case 4

Cathy's basic organic integrity and basic ego functions were age-appropriate, as indicated by the level, depth, and organization of personal relatedness; the organization, depth, and richness of affects and themes; and the stability of her mood.

Her flexibility of ego structure was, for the most part, at an age-appropriate level in that during her interview she demonstrated a wide-ranging, rich development of age-appropriate relatedness, affects, and themes with no indications of disruptive anxiety or marked limitations of either positive or negative affects and themes. For example, she engaged the interviewer easily and demonstrated initial concern with the limits of the playroom—in a sense asking if she could give in to her instincts—which is very appropriate behavior for late Oedipal to early latency-stage children (i.e., the tension between letting go versus control).

While the concerns with cleanliness versus messing with the salt indicated some conflict, she was able to elaborate these concerns and use them as a take off for an ever-deepening series of communications that touched on themes of exploration, competition (with mother), anger (at brother), and feelings of loss and separation. Near the end of the interview she demonstrated a growing age-appropriate curiosity and seductiveness, indicating that there was "more" she could tell me. There may be one aspect of rigidity in her personality structure—a kind of pseudo maturity and joviality around issues of some importance to her, such as her relationship with her brother. She may be slightly overinvested in her competition with her mother as well. These are subtleties in her drama, however, which in themselves do not detract from the fundamental structural integrity and flexibility of her personality.

Her concerns consisted of a variety of age-appropriate issues ranging across negative and positive affects and across Oedipal and early latency themes.

### Formulations for Case 5

In this case we observe suggestions of severe compromises in the organic integrity of ego functioning, as evidenced by the immature gross and fine motor integration, speech, gait, posturing, intermittent perseveration, and overall concrete style of relating. Further testing, including psychological and neurological examinations, would provide important additional data. It would be important to make certain that these severe compromises were not due primarily to anxiety.

The basic ego functions are also seriously compromised, as we observe impairments in regulation of impulses and activity level. A capacity for human relationships is clearly present but severely constricted, as evidenced by the only fleeting and somewhat impersonal concrete way the patient related to the interviewer. While reality testing was intact in a global sense, one would wonder about the potential for regression in reality testing under

159

stress, as evidenced in the "blank look" and rocking on the floor (which may have been a response to anxiety). The narrow range and depth of affect suggest compromises in the flexibility of the personality. The constricted range and depth of thematic communication are further evidence of severe constriction.

The overall organization of themes, while not reflecting fragmentation or highly idiosyncratic forms suggestive of a functional psychotic organization, did reflect a much more immature level (a 3- to 4-year-old level) than would be expected in a 6½-year-old. This immaturity (e.g., islands of thematic concerns rather than cohesive, rich thematic organizations) may be related to an immature capacity for integration based on the compromises in the organic integrity of ego functioning.

We observe a vulnerable ego structure that operates very inflexibly. Nevertheless, we may still observe hints of this child's concerns. After feeling out of control, he attempts to regain control through perseveration and making contact with the interviewer. Frustrated, he becomes angry and out of control again. Yet there are the ambivalent feelings toward the "policeman," again suggesting a desire for regulation and at the same time anger at the source of such regulation. Frightened at his ambivalent ("bad boy") feelings, there is a momentary loss of relatedness followed by rocking movements. He recovers, however, makes contact again, asking for candy, but then once again becomes angry and out of control. His ability briefly to relate events at school suggests that these concerns permeate his life.

We observe, therefore, how he struggles to deal with his very vulnerable ego functions. The existence of conflicts suggests the basis of motivation for treatment.

### Formulations for Case 6

Both the organic and functional aspects of David's ego structure were age-appropriate, as evinced by his physical and neurological functioning, the quality of his relatedness, his stable mood, and the level of organization of his affects and themes. The flexibility of his personality also seemed entirely age-appropriate. Although one might expect a little more repression of Oedipal concerns by this age, I was quite impressed with his ability to make warm contact with me. During the interview he demonstrated a variety of emotions. He developed a cohesive, organized theme through play with dolls, modulating the emotions of the different characters he created. When his "story" aroused anxiety, he moved on to other—but related—games and themes. Similarly, he showed flexibility in his affect system, though with some limitations.

His main concerns were with anger and not getting enough, although in his interpersonal contact with me he demonstrated the capacity for pleasure and enjoyment as well. While there were concerns with developmentally early (pre-Oedipal) affects, I would guess that these are in an age-appropriate (Oedipal) context. He showed a capacity for a wide variety of affects and did not rely on primitive defenses such as denial, avoidance, and projection; instead, he was able to deal directly with the themes and affects concerning him. In addition, he seemed clever and intelligent, and was able to synthesize, organize, and integrate his material very well. He regulated his behavior in accord with the limits of the playroom (i.e., there was no difficulty with impulse control). He dealt with themes of anger in a displaced way through games. His capacity for pleasure and enjoyment indicated good self-esteem. His talk about not getting enough Coke did not seem to be accompanied by a sense of true depression; rather, it seemed more related to age-appropriate wishes. While there was overall age-appropriate flexibility, there are questions of minor limitations, as indicated both by the absence of more direct themes of pleasure and curiosity and by the subjective feelings of the interviewer regarding limitations in the emotional level of relatedness.

His special concerns were reflected in his dramatic rendering of an elaborate family drama, which took up a major part of the session. He was concerned with "things falling off," competition, and being replenished. He may be quite enmeshed in these concerns, trying with some difficulty to gain distance from them in order to resolve them. The question of ego flexibility would seem to depend on how well he works through an intense Oedipal involvement, but there do not seem to be any prominent or major ego restrictions to hamper his resolution. What happens in his family at this time may play a critical role in this resolution. How his family deals with him will in part determine whether he continues developing in an optimal, age-appropriate way.

## Formulations for Case 7

With respect to Joey's basic ego functions, neurological integrity was at the age-appropriate level, as indicated by the quality and level of his motor activity. He seemed relaxed and calm, and his fine and gross motor coordination as well as his perceptual-motor ability and coordination all seemed intact. There was a slight lisp to his speech, which was nevertheless understandable.

While reality testing seemed age-appropriate, as did impulse control and affect regulation, there appeared to be a lack of full object constancy in that we did not see if he could function without mother. It was as though he were one step behind the age-appropriate developmental level in his human relationship capacities; flirting, so to speak, with the issues of power and size (phallic issues) but too involved with his dyadic tie to mother to do more than that. His unresolved individuation from mother seems to be intensified by age-appropriate Oedipal feelings alongside dependent, aggressive, angry, and manipulative themes. He seemed infantile and babyish even with the playful expressions he enjoyed vis-à-vis manipulating mother, who seemed to play right into his hands. I would therefore raise questions about the age-appropriate integrity of the basic ego structure in the line of development related to relationships.

His ego seemed quite rigid, as indicated by his need to maintain the attachment to mother in the playroom, his inability to explore the playroom, his limited ability to relate to me during the course of the interview, and the lack of development of rich themes or organized play. On the positive side, he did elaborate a number of themes and was able to dramatize some of his conflicts around aggression, his tie to mother, his feeling little, and his experience of danger. I felt all this elaboration was in a rather limited context, however.

Predominant affects demonstrated in the interview were apprehension, separation anxiety, and anger, with a facade of playful and pleasurable manipulativeness around the issue of control. The affects thus seemed predominantly representative of earlier age levels (i.e., not at a full Oedipal level). The newness of the situation should not be overlooked, however; he may be capable of other, more flexible affects in a situation familiar to him. Because there seemed to be a hint of warmth and interest in me, as well as some flexibility in the affects as the interview proceeded, there may be some hidden potential in the area of affects; in general, however, the affects seemed rather fixed, rigid, and limited to the pre-Oedipal level.

Joey's anxiety seemed to center on separation, with some concerns around being engulfed orally (e.g., the little dog being eaten up), and perhaps some castration anxiety (as evinced by the shooting). Internal signal anxieties did not appear to be fully operable yet in this child's development.

He used avoidance, attempting to avoid me and the playroom situation by a kind of regressive dependent clinging to his mother (it appears from the history that he has been able to go to nursery school and to separate from her at other times). He also made use of projection, as indicated by the degree of fear and apprehension he experienced with regard to the playroom.

He seemed quite apprehensive and frightened of me; he was not prepared to use me in any way as a triangular figure in his life. Although it is possible that he is in a "hot" Oedipal situation, and therefore feels quite frightened of me insofar as I represent the father, I felt that his apprehension stemmed from a lack of *secure* object constancy (i.e., a secure sense of self and a sure grasp of the division between self and others). That he has accomplished this division to some degree was suggested by his general capacity for age-appropriate reality testing and by his ability to regulate affects and impulses. He has not mastered it to the extent expected in a 5-year-old, however; object constancy is a vulnerable area that causes him to regress under stress. His concerns fell somewhere between the pre-Oedipal and Oedipal levels.

He has not fully established himself in an Oedipal configuration—it appeared to frighten him. It was as though he were saying, "I am interested in size, power, and competition, and I want to use my gun" (all early phallic concerns, which lie at the early end of his current developmental phase). At the same time, he did not yet feel secure in his delineation of self. Therefore, he used manipulative devices to maintain a playful, seductive, but dependent tie to mother. From a structural point of view, such devices indicate his lack of readiness for real age-appropriate concerns. Joey therefore employs a stage and a drama that are both one level below his expected developmental level.

## Formulations for Case 8

From the interview data alone it appeared that Mark's basic ego functions were disordered and far below age expectations. The capacities that one would expect to see in a 4½-year-old (i.e., impulse regulation, reality testing, and the capacity to organize affect and thematic communications) were lacking in this child. Rather, as indicated earlier, in terms of these basic ego functions, Mark seemed to be functioning more like a 1- to

2-year-old and, at that, a 1- to 2-year-old who was on a disordered pathway. For example, a healthy 15-month-old child can develop organized nonverbal play themes, something this child could not do. Although one would want further data from psychological testing, one might hypothesize that Mark's intellectual functioning is actually at the appropriate age level, as evinced by his capacities to spell and name objects. His ability to use his intellect to organize his social and emotional pursuits, however, would appear to be highly compromised by the severe disruption in his basic ego functions, as outlined above.

He seemed to be struggling with the most fundamental issues of early development—namely, the abilities to organize communication, to begin modulating some of his impulses, to begin integrating some aspects of positive and negative feelings, and to begin a better integration of motor functioning and sensorimotor coordination. One would expect a child to achieve such developmental tasks by the end of his second year of life. On the basis of this initial playroom interview, therefore, one would recommend a thorough neurological examination. It would not be surprising, however, if such examination revealed only subtle, soft signs, as already evinced by his clumsiness; the major findings would be the severe lag in social and emotional development. From this perspective, much of Mark's functioning was below the level of a 2-year-old, whose developmental tasks center on themes of separation, modulation of aggressive impulses, organization of communication patterns, stabilization of mood, and development of purposeful initiative.

To round out the evaluation of such a child one would certainly need a detailed developmental history, psychological testing, and a neurological exam. The clinical interview data alone, however, were enough to indicate serious compromises in all aspects of basic ego functioning.

### Formulations for Case 9

*First Interview*

My impression was that the physical and neurological components of Molly's ego functioning were basically intact. There were no obvious signs of disorganization or fragmentation: she showed a reality orientation to the playroom; she modulated and regulated her impulses; she organized her themes. There was no highly inappropriate affect, but at the same time, the degree of her inhibition, coupled with the severe constriction of her affect, made one wonder if there were some fine cracks in the basic ego functions. Molly's drama was evinced in her affect hunger, constriction, and inhibition around age-appropriate themes.

With respect to the flexibility of her basic personality patterns, we observed an extraordinarily rigid little girl, especially for one 4½ years old. One expects rich, complex, organized affects and themes from a child of that age; instead, we saw severe rigidity. Again, the question that should be raised is, was this constriction covering some below age-appropriate basic ego functioning? Were there some fine cracks in the structure?

Because there was some question in my mind after the first interview about whether Molly was functioning with characterological constrictions or whether some basic ego functions were indeed well below the age-appropriate level, I conducted a second diagnostic interview (this is often a useful procedure).

*Second Interview*

During the second interview Molly showed that the hypothesis of "fine cracks in the basic ego functions" suggested by the first interview was not, in fact, the case. She showed that she possessed a greater capacity and range of affect, thematic involvement, and relatedness than she originally revealed. She did, however, confirm the presence of a fundamental constriction in the flexibility of her personality. She continued to communicate in a restrictive, depressed way; her mood was tense, and she showed a restricted range of affects. She developed her themes of aggression in a deep and rich fashion—showing her preoccupation with aggressiveness—and was not involved in the more pleasurable, curious, and sexual aspects of her development, which would have been appropriate for her age.

The drama that she was dealing with in the context of her inflexible and constricted ego structure revealed itself more clearly during the second interview. She was, in fact, preoccupied with themes of aggression. She made it clear that she was concerned with hurting and being hurt; that she saw her emerging femininity as caught up in this aggressive theme and therefore too laden with conflict to handle; and that she was quite uncomfortable with the picture of herself as a "poisonous snake." She associated the snake picture with a fear of being overwhelmed and "not breathing," but took reassurance from a demanding, *concrete* connectedness with the significant others in her life.

Therefore, in summary, we see a picture of a 4½-year-old girl whose ego functioning is already highly constricted and whose conflicts center on very primitive themes of aggression, being overwhelmed, and losing important objects in her life.

### Formulations for Case 10

There are questions about the age-appropriate integrity of some of Eddie's basic ego functions. Although he showed no gross disorientation in his overall age-expected reality testing, his capacity to organize thinking at an age-appropriate level did seem compromised, as shown by his negotiation of the playroom. Similarly, although he showed no overt signs of impulse control problems, one would wonder whether he has difficulty controlling his impulses in other settings, given his preoccupation during the interview with twisting off the dolls' arms and otherwise hurting the dolls. Given these observations plus the poverty of the range and depth of his symbolic communications (themes), one might postulate that Eddie's emerging self-image is itself compromised in terms of being an organizational unit that provides stability for basic personality functions such as reality testing, impulse regulation, mood stabilization, and an ever-growing delineation of self from nonself. Again, the fact that we did not see any major disruptions in these personality functions indicated, to some degree, their age-appropriate integrity.

Nevertheless, this 3½-year-old boy functioned well below his age level in subtler capacities, such as organizing communication and affect, and expressing a richness and depth of affect. Thus, we see that he is already using major characterological constrictions to hold together what would appear to be a fragile personality organization. That he was so tense and apprehensive, showed such a narrow range of affect, and only meagerly developed his themes all suggest the degree to which his personality structure is significantly "walled off."

Observations of the thematic sequence and type of affect gave a picture of some of his developmental concerns. He has been struggling with his ambivalence, and particularly with his angry feelings, trying to integrate them into some ongoing relationship with the human world. He certainly has not given up on the human world; indeed, he is beginning to work out a compromise that features a pattern of mildly impersonal relatedness. This allowed him to stand close to the interviewer without any real sense of investment or interest. In sum, we see a child who is invested in the world and who possesses some age-appropriate capacities. In certain other areas, however, he is far below age expectations. He presents a picture of uneven ego development.

### Formulations for Case 11

The physical and neurological aspects of Molly's basic ego functions seemed intact, as indicated by her gross and fine motor activity, language ability, and overall intellectual skills (evinced by her capacity to name the letters and pick the correct letter for her sister's name, copy circles, etc.). She also showed an overall awareness of what was going on and exhibited a capacity to follow instructions and to focus her attention in an extraordinarily effective manner in the course of the play.

With regard to the psychological aspects of basic ego functions, Jane seemed at an age-appropriate level in her ability to organize her thematic communication, even though she was slightly immature in that she had only islands of thematic organization. She presented her descriptions and occasional interactive themes in a cohesive, organized way. Her affect, while chronically anxious and apprehensive, was nonetheless well organized and integrated with her thematic presentation. She also displayed a fundamental capacity for a relatedness infused with personal warmth; her relatedness was in the age-appropriate range. Her self-modulated activity level, impulse control, and understanding of the situation were all consistent with age-appropriate capacities. As indicated, her mood was stable, albeit constricted in range. Jane's basic ego functions, therefore, seemed to be at an age-appropriate level.

In terms of her flexibility, however, she showed a number of marked constrictions not appropriate for her age, particularly with regard to the range of affect. We would expect that Jane—being close to 3 years old—would demonstrate gleeful pleasure, assertiveness, curiosity, and, in the appropriate situation, signs of aggression or negativism, all in the symbolic and representational mode. Jane showed little of this affective range. Although some mild aggressiveness was seen in the interactive play with the fish, the affect accompanying it was weak and pale. Of even greater concern, there were few signs of joyful pleasure, and while there was some capacity for exploring and moving around the room, here, too, there seemed to be some constriction. In addition, the affects were not developed in a deep, rich manner consistent with age expectations.

167

Similarly, her thematic development lacked range and her themes lacked richness and depth. As a child moves from age 2 to 3, one should see a greater capacity than Jane showed to use the representational mode to convey inner feelings, thoughts, wishes, and organized fantasies; this development parallels a readiness to depart from the strictly descriptive level wherein the child names objects. This developmental progression was not evident in Jane's communications with her mother, which were permeated with apprehension and a generally tense quality. Jane's preference for the descriptive level was more consistent with the style of a 2- to 2½-year-old than with that of an almost 3-year-old. In sum, the flexibility of the personality was markedly below age-appropriate capacity, resembling that of a tense and anxious 2- to 2½-year-old.

With respect to this child's concerns, we can only speculate about what might be responsible for the constriction in thematic and affective range and depth. We saw that both she and mother seemed to be chronically apprehensive and tense, and that when Jane experimented with aggression, taking the fish to bite mother, mother quickly turned the tables. Although mother smiled (superficially and tensely) and tried to make this turnabout part of the game, her "quick trigger" suggested to me that she was not comfortable with Jane's emerging capacity for organized assertiveness and exploration and their aggressive components. Additional supportive evidence for this possibility was Jane's tendency to stay physically close to mother and hold onto her, as opposed to being more comfortable with the explorativeness that would accompany her otherwise confident cognitive development. Though a fundamental warmth was evident in their relatedness, so was an underlying uneasiness. Regarding separation, explorativeness, and aggression, it would seem that at one time in their relationship there was a greater capacity for shared pleasure, which is now on more tenuous grounds, caught up in anxiety.

In summary, then, we see a child of 2 years and 11 months whose basic ego functions are intact, but who seems to have severe constrictions in age-appropriate flexibility of personality functions and perhaps is conflicted and concerned with the issues of separation, assertion, and aggression. Using our metaphor, Jane's stage is structurally intact in its physical, neurological, and psychological ego functions, but it is already developing some major constrictions. These constrictions are probably responsible for some of the symptoms that caused this child to be brought in for the evaluation.

The interview was conducted with the mother in the playroom because the child was so young. I did not try to have Jane come in alone, although she might have been able to, particularly after spending some time with me and her mother in the waiting room. With children this young, one learns a great deal about the child by watching its interactions with mother. Jane's interview thus differs from the interviews of the older children presented here, where the children were in the playroom with me alone. Nonetheless, as this description may indicate, there is much to observe about children with their mothers during this age period, which may then be compared to age-appropriate capacities.

## Concluding Remarks

In concluding this section on formulation, brief mention should again be made of the fact that, in routine clinical care settings, the clinical interview is but one of many sources of data one uses in arriving at a formulation. The foregoing discussion demonstrates the degree to which the clinical interview can be the cornerstone of the formulation. Notwithstanding that observational data derived from the interview setting can be used for arriving at good clinical hypotheses, additional data are always necessary. For example, in most instances, psychological testing provides valuable information that will enhance one's capacity to make clinical judgments and develop appropriate formulations. It is interesting to note that the observational categories described earlier may also be used to organize the data that emerge from psychological test reports. For example, the findings of the Bender Visual Motor Gestalt Test and various intelligence tests provide very useful data about the physical and neurological integrity of the central nervous system. Subtle lags in instrumental or conceptual cognitive abilities can be picked up through these tests. Data from the Rorschach will occasionally expose a child's covert difficulties in distinguishing fantasy from reality (assuming this distinction is age-appropriate). Responses to the Rorschach, as well as to the TAT and various figure-drawing exercises, also provide exceedingly valuable data on the level of personality development and the types of concerns and/or conflicts a child is experiencing. Indeed, psychological testing can provide important findings regarding all three of the questions we have examined in this chapter: (1) the basic integrity of the personality structure, as evinced by the level of basic organic and psychological ego functions; (2) the flexibility of the personality; and (3) the child's specific concerns and conflicts.

One point should be stressed, however. When conducting a full evaluation, a clinician should optimally have specific questions in mind to ask via the psychological testing. In other words, if done systematically and logically, the clinical interview will provide first-order information that raises hypotheses with varying degrees of certainty. (Some questions arise that are more in the nature of hunches than hypotheses.) For example, from the clinical interview one may have questions about whether there is a lag in perceptual-motor integration because the child showed some delay in fine motor coordination and some lack of clarity in speech. Thus a specific question will be formulated for clarification by the diagnostic psychological testing.

Similarly, we may see a child who seems to have good organization of affect and age-appropriate thematic organization but who, once or twice during the interview, seems to bring in a theme from out of left field, or who demonstrates some affects that are far below age expectations or otherwise inappropriate. In such cases, psychological testing might provide valuable insights about a subtle lag in the child's capacity for age-appropriate differentiation of internal and external experience (fantasy from reality).

Another example is the child who comes across in the interview as unduly polarized, with extreme personality rigidities, and who shows only the passive domain of human experience. Psychological testing may be able to reveal whether a hidden vulnerability or weakness in the fabric of the personality structure underlies this seeming characterological constriction, or whether in different circumstances the child shows greater variation and flexibility in the range of experience.

While traditional psychological testing (including intelligence tests, Rorschachs, TATs, and Bender Visual Motor Gestalt Tests) involves many unstructured exercises (e.g., the Rorschach), it complements the unstructured clinical interview in an important way. Even the most unstructured components of the routine battery employ standard stimuli, and the responses of many children to these stimuli have been studied. Therefore, in addition to enabling us to study certain areas of personality functioning (such as intellectual functioning) in greater depth than is possible in the clinical interview, testing also offers an opportunity to see how a child deals with these standard stimuli.

The above remarks are intended only as passing comments on psychological testing; the present context does not allow a full discussion of all the complex issues that could be raised. The point I want to emphasize, however, is that in a systematic clinical evaluation, the clinical interview should be used as the basis or framework for raising questions. Optimally, clinicians ask highly specific questions via psychological testing, even though they must also be prepared to hear answers to questions that they did not raise.

There are other sources of data that complement the data that emerge from the clinical interview. For example, where there are questions about conceptual or instrumental aspects of intellectual functioning, specialized testing may be appropriate; such testing may range from hearing tests to tests for specific perceptual-motor difficulties, to tests for particular processing difficulties in the verbal or temporal-spatial areas. Furthermore, information from the child's regular and special school teachers, as well as information from others who are an important part of the child's life (e.g., at religious school, special clubs, and other activities), are all valuable sources of data, particularly when the clinical interview raises difficult questions.

In this work, we will not be able to consider these other sources of information. We will, however, briefly consider information that one should routinely obtain from parents about parental and family functioning as well as the child's developmental history.

# Chapter 7

# Interviewing the Parents: Selected Comments

This chapter will discuss aspects of the clinical interview with the parents, including: observing each parent's personality organization, noting family patterns, obtaining a developmental history, conveying your recommendations, and helping parents deal with resistances and/or other factors that may interfere with their "hearing" or following through on your recommendations. These subjects will not be discussed comprehensively. Rather, some suggestions on selected aspects of interviewing the parents will be covered.

### Assessing the Parents

The same basic method that we used to assess the child will be used to assess the parents, namely, systematic observations made during an unstructured interview. These firsthand observations constitute the most reliable information you can get about the parents, so you must make the most of the interview period by way of facilitating communication. It is especially important during the opening moments not to lead the parents. During this initial phase, focus first on the parents as individuals, observing each person as a clinical entity, and focus second on their relationship.

Using the same principles used in the interview with the child, I try to let the parents start the interview while I listen. At the beginning of the typical interview, I will be warm and clearly available; I make eye contact, smile, nod or shake hands when appropriate, and then look expectant. I assume that the parents know why they are here and I will not patronize them, even inadvertently, by structuring the beginning. In these circumstances most people wish to, and will, structure things for themselves. They will say, for example, that the reason they have come is that Johnny is having problems in school, or Sally is having nightmares and disturbing the whole family, or some such broad statement. If they look anxious for some moments as they greet me and sit down, I will patiently allow them time to organize their thoughts rather than doing it for them. I will not say, e.g., "Well, obviously you've come to tell me about Johnny. You've already told me on the phone . . ." Rather, I want to see what the parents do with the situation.

Depending on the situation, I might say, e.g., "You are looking at me very expectantly," to which they could respond, "We were thinking you might have a lot of questions." Then I might say, "I probably will, but I don't know where to begin. I'd like to hear from you first." Given permission in this way, they will be off and running. If they seem especially anxious in the first few minutes I might say, e.g., "Sometimes it's hard to get one's thoughts together in a situation like this," which may serve to relax them and help them organize their thinking without deflecting attention from the purpose of the interview.

The parents usually begin with something related to the child. But they may begin with family issues, their discomfort about coming to see you, or more tangential issues. They may start with one sentence about the child and then switch to their own parents or some problems at work; 10 minutes later you still have not heard anything more about the child. Rather than interrupting or bringing them back to their starting point, it is preferable in such circumstances to follow the parents' natural associative trends.

For example, the father may be talking about some argument he had with his boss. Listen carefully to this aggressive theme and ask yourself if it is related to how the parents feel about coming to see you. You may hypothesize that they are expecting some competition or rivalry. If the parental theme focuses on being humiliated, the parents may be fearful of exposing something. Alternatively, if they have never talked to a psychiatrist before, they may have some unusual ideas about what is going to happen, such as a fantasy that they are going to tell you about their child and you are going to take the child away and lock him up. If you feel some strong affect at the beginning, or if the opening moves are not in the range that you usually encounter, it is worthwhile to ask an open-ended question that plays back in a supportive way—not in an intrusive or guilt-provoking way—what you have noticed.

The amount of work you have to do at the beginning of the interview says something about the family structure. Highly tangential material offered at the beginning of the interview may reflect resistance and fearfulness. Often your supportive feedback can help some anxiety to emerge and thus make it easier for parents to tell their story. Let me emphasize, however, that you make such comments only after you have had an opportunity to observe the parents for a few minutes and have listened to the content and sequence of their associative trends. In this way you will get a clear picture of the issues the parents are trying to deal with and thus be able to form questions or comments which more precisely reflect their concerns.

For example, a couple came to see me about a young adolescent boy. They looked at each other, they looked at me, and I looked back. We went through an uncomfortable few moments which allowed quick access to the fact that they did not easily give me anything, as they did not give much to their teenage son. Eventually it emerged that the parents were very depressed: they were caught up in marital problems and rarely talked to each other; the father was also having terrible troubles at work. Having heard about these issues, I was then able to ask specific questions that would help them tell their story.

To assess the parents in this initial phase, I use the same categories that I described earlier for observing children. That is, I observe their physical makeup, neurological integrity, gross and fine motor systems, sensory modalities, speech, activity levels, etc. Then I observe their mood and affects; the way they organize their thinking, communications, and affects; and how they tell their story. From all these observations I learn something about their personality structures and can make a good guess as to their degree of pathology; that is, whether they are in the neurotic range, the characterological range, or the borderline psychotic range.

In addition to observing each parent individually, it is important to see how they relate to each other and how, as a team, they relate to you. You want to look at who dominates, how they share in telling their concerns. Watching the evolution of their story can give you some answers. For instance, without much instruction, some parents can give you a rich, organized history of the family and impression of the child's problem. These people show you that they operate together in a fairly organized, cohesive manner. Other parents, in contrast, may keep undermining one another, causing the history of the child's difficulties to evolve in a fragmented, disorganized way. Tangential thinking gives you a picture of a disorganized family environment.

It is also important to observe their perceptions of one another. For example, take a case where the wife saw the husband as a big tyrant (he was, in fact, 6'4") and herself as a helpless, dependent little thing who could run the family only by stealthy manipulation because she could not deal directly with his explosiveness. The couple had stereotyped images of one another, which were based on their experiences with their own families. After further discussion, it turned out that the father actually felt very dependent and insecure and was frightened that his wife would leave him. In fact, after a series of interviews it emerged that the mother realized she had the power in the family. She became aware that she identified to some degree with her own father, who was a very strong figure in her family, and that she had taken on certain of his controlling characteristics. As this couple saw that their perceptions of one another were partly based on projections of certain stereotyped images, they became more flexible in the way they related to each other. It was useful to understand these projections because both were also projecting a denied part of their selves onto their son, who had psychosomatic difficulties.

Third, it is important to look at the specific way each parent relates to, and what each feels about, the child. Often you can pick this up by letting each parent describe the child's problem without your asking many questions. Listen to their associative trends. In particular, you want to look for distorted perceptions, which play an important role in the child's pathology.

For example, a frequent syndrome I have seen with adolescent boys is the father who sees the teenager as a threat (a revival of Oedipal issues). Afraid of his own aggression, the father remains somewhat distant and aloof. Mother, on the other hand, sees the child as a passive, dependent thing whom she needs to nurture. The parents paint two very different pictures: one talks about the child as helpless and dependent, and the other talks

175

about the child as an aggressive monster. Although quite discordant, these may be firmly fixed perceptions.

Of particular interest is to what degree these distorted perceptions of the child reflect displacements from problems that the parents are having with one another. Frequently the child becomes the receptacle for problems that the parents cannot work out. Mother may have some impulses that she would like to relate to father but cannot, and instead deflects them onto the child. Father may feel quite angry at and threatened by mother, and may deflect these feelings onto the child.

In one family, for example, mother had a lot of frustrated Oedipal wishes. She was somewhat insecure in her ability to take an assertive, affectionate role with her husband, seeing him as aloof, withdrawn, and absorbed in his legal practice. She was always complaining that he did not pay attention to her. Meanwhile, when it came time to make love, she was always a little withdrawn and would find excuses. Mother defended against some of her warm feelings toward her husband by seeing him as cold, aloof, and uninterested, and then transferred some of the warmth of her own instinctual interest onto her 5-year-old boy. Her discomfort with this pure Oedipal situation, however, involved her in heated, intense power struggles with this child. Here one can see that mother perceived her husband as cold (he was actually much warmer than she thought) in order to protect herself against her feelings. She used the child as the object of some of her feelings. The child's response to the struggle was to hold onto his feces (having bowel movements about once every 10 days) and show negativism. He was basically locked, both characterologically and instinctually, into an anal pattern, even though there were some signs that he had reached an Oedipal phase of development.

In such a situation, it is important to see that a child is more than a victim; he or she may have played an important role in initiating the family pattern. By the time children are 5 or 6, they have their own needs and intentions and may take advantage of a particular family situation to promote these. In some families where the parents are having difficulties, one child will get right in the middle and want to solve all their problems, while another will say, "The heck with it, let them struggle" and tune out of the family in favor of greater involvement with school and friends. To be sure, even the latter child suffers some effects of the parental dynamics, but they may have less impact and stay with him for a shorter period of time because he does not essentially "buy into" them. In other words, he does not see parental difficulties as an opportunity to satisfy some of his instinctual needs. He thinks the parental battles are a little crazy and confusing, and more or less tunes them out, seeking to meet certain needs elsewhere.

In looking at the parents' conscious and unconscious perceptions of the child it is important to learn how these views relate to the child's developmental stage. Although some parents have fixed, distorted perceptions of the child, these may nevertheless be helpful to the child at a particular developmental phase. The father who sees his young son as a narcissistic extension of his own athletic abilities may be helpful to him when the child is learning certain latency-age skills, but impede the child's strivings in other phases of development.

The engulfing mother who sees all children as helpless and dependent may be an excellent parent in the first months of her child's life, since infants basically need a special kind of love and care. However, when the child gets to be 12–16 months old and starts walking around the house, wanting to explore and separate, you may see such a mother continually undermining both the child's exploratory activities and his sense of mastery or real separation from her. The mother's undermining may take one of numerous forms, such as anger, control, or manipulation, all of which serve to keep the child at an infantile level, thus feeding her own dependency hunger.

In families where the mother and father are not living together, each one can still offer support in the treatment process. There may also be other family members—or surrogate family members—who are crucial to the child. Have them come in and contribute to the initial diagnostic process by sharing their impression of the child; they can be helpful not only as informants but also as supports of the child during treatment. For instance, you may want to involve a neighborhood friend who is the major babysitter for the 5-year-old while mother works. Although you need to work clinically through the mother, this surrogate mother definitely needs to be taken into account.

In summary, during the first part of the interview, focus your attention on structural personality issues and family dynamics. Do not be too concerned with whether the parents get right to the point of why they called. If they start off on a tangent, let that go on for a while because it will give you a good picture of what kind of people they are and how they relate to one another. Be on the lookout for parental perceptions and possible distortions in the context of the child's age-appropriate developmental activities. One or both parents may have a character disorder or some neurotic configurations that distort the way the child is perceived. Then, after the first 20 minutes or so, you may want to move in and structure the interview in order to get a more detailed picture of what is going on in the family and of the current problems and overall development of the child in question.

## The Presenting Problem

Follow up whatever statements the parents have made about why they came to see you with questions that elicit a clear picture of the child's current problems. Ask for examples of each and every problem and inquire about its manifestation in all the child's environments: at school, at home, on the block with friends, and so on.

Find out exactly when each problem began and what precipitated it— e.g., a family crisis, a certain event, the child's (or his family's) conflicts about his development.

Your goal is to obtain a brief history and complete cross-sectional picture of the "present illness." Thus you require details about the child's current functioning and his functioning just before the precipitating crisis *in each area outlined in the categories of Chapter 2.* A detailed knowledge of the child's functioning across the board requires great patience and systematic focusing (i.e., each category). It will, however, tell you about *all* the problem areas and their contexts. This sort of detailed history is crucial to your fully understanding not only the current problems, their likely precipitants, and their pervasiveness, but also the related strengths and vulnerabilities that the child possesses. Often the most significant issue is not part of the presenting problem.

## Taking the History

In addition to the routine questions one asks in taking a history to elicit information in the biological, physical, and nutritional realms, you must also obtain information about the child's psychological development. Now parents vary in their ability to be good historians, particularly with regard to this latter aspect of their child's life. You can help by asking the right kinds of questions.

Your questioning should facilitate an understanding of how the child came to be the way he is, i.e., what constitutional and/or experiential, etiological factors, were involved. The clinician who knows how normal

178

development progresses should be able to discover whether the child always had certain tendencies, or whether he functioned well and then suddenly regressed. By obtaining data relevant to each of the observational categories (see Chapter 2) from birth onward, you will have a picture of when the child's problems began and perhaps some clues about what caused them. The developmental tables in Chapter 3 are useful in this context; they show both the range of normal behavior for each age group and the important developmental milestones. Proceed systematically from the time of birth through each 6-month period up to age 4, then look at the changes occurring in each year up to the present age of the child. For each period you want to make sure you know something about the neurological and physiological aspects, the psychological development, the interpersonal development, and important events in the family's life. As you can well imagine, taking a history properly may require more than one session. Begin your history-taking with a sketch of the family tree in terms of the presence or absence of mental illness, learning disorders, and chronic physical illnesses. Then inquire about the mother's prenatal experiences, finding out about nutrition, drugs, emotional stress, her feelings and her husband's about the pregnancy. Ask, too, about their experience of the birth process itself.

Although you want to know something about each area of development as outlined in Table 1, there are certain basic developmental tasks on which you can focus your questions. To begin with, one should get an impression of the baby's capacity to establish the basic homeostatic patterns early in life. The key issues here are regulation of and interest in the world, which depend in part on the maturity of the baby's central nervous system and/or special sensitivities or hyperreactions to auditory, visual, and tactile stimuli. Some babies quiet down as soon as they see the mother or hear her voice. Other babies need to be rocked in just the right way and given optimum care to reach a stage of equilibrium. In the latter case you want to understand the cause of the child's hypersensitivity: for example, was there an immaturity in the child's central nervous system? Or might the child have been colicky, with an allergy to dairy products? Ask about the baby's environment as well. In sum, you want to get a picture of the initial organization of the central nervous system, which is indicated in part by the infant's ability to establish organized patterns, to interrelate these patterns with mother's patterns, to regulate the self, and to become engaged in the world by being alert for reasonable periods of time.

Much research has been done on early developmental differences. For instance, T. Berry Brazelton (1973) has been interested in the baby's constitutional status and has developed a neonatal assessment profile to discover individual differences among infants. His work has greatly refined the concept of temperament. Although none of the research is predictive in any sense, it is suggestive and certainly enables us to ask better questions than in the past, making it worthwhile to have some familiarity with this literature (see Greenspan, in press).

Continuing with the newborn phase, you also want to get a feeling for the mother's response to the infant and vice versa. First, was there an attachment formed between the two, and what was the quality of the attachment? You want to see the richness and depth of that capacity to form an attachment, the kind of emotions, and whether the mother's feelings were predominantly negative or positive.

If an attachment was formed and you know something about the quality of it, next find out about the quality of the infant's beginning capacity to differentiate. The infant's attachment to mother forms the foundation from which the infant can begin differentiating his or her self as a distinct entity from the nurturing figure. You want to look at this capacity for differentiation in terms of both the motoric elements of the sensorimotor system and the human elements—that is, the baby's capacity to see the mother as a distinct person with whom to interact and from whom to get feedback. Differentiation is the process you see when the mother holds a young child close and the child pushes away to look at the mother. You want to get a picture of what that process was like for this particular child. Was this a mother who, every time the child pushed back to get a better look, held the child in because she felt rejected? Or was this a mother who, as soon as the child showed any curiosity, threw the child off her lap and said, "There, go it alone"?

The capacity for balanced empathy on the part of the nurturing figure —that is, the ability to be indulgent, giving, loving, and protective, and at the same time to experience emotionally something of what the infant experiences—is essential. A mother with balanced empathy is both in tune with her infant and able to distinguish her own needs from her infant's needs. The mother who consistently projects onto the infant and smothers him with care may be good for the first couple of months, but may make it hard for the infant when he begins to differentiate in the middle of his first year.

Toward the end of the first year of life, one of the infant's major developmental tasks is to learn to distinguish between and differentiate the different people in the environment; particularly, to learn the difference between the people who have been giving him primary care versus other people. Stranger anxiety is only *one* of many possible signs of that capacity. Some infants show almost no stranger anxiety and yet have highly integrated differentiating capacities which early in life include an unusually high degree of trust. These babies might have an excessive smile for mother rather than a fear or anxiety for the stranger. On the other hand, extreme stranger anxiety may represent a good deal of tension in the infant. Most important is to determine if enough differentiation occurred for the infant to engage in reciprocal communication patterns (e.g., purposeful, causal interactions) in a range of emotional domains. In your history-taking with the parents, you want to get a picture of how the child fared at learning these early developmental tasks.

You want to find out if, as the child began his second year of life, he developed more organized behavioral and emotional patterns; how he negotiated the beginning of the separation process; and if he was capable of new and original behavior. Piaget (1969) refers to this developmental stage as the tertiary circular reactions. Mahler (1975) talks about it in terms of the practicing subphase of separation-individuation. That is, between 10 and 16 months, as the infant develops greater motor ability, he or she begins to explore the environment with a sense of omnipotent grandeur: the toddler becomes king or queen of the universe. The infant toddles around the house, separating from the parent under what Mahler calls "the omnipotent umbrella": still feeling as though he is a part of the parent even though he can distinguish himself from the parent.

In this phase, the baby should be demonstrating imitative behavior and dealing with the world in an organized way. He begins to internalize, organize, and take initiative in the environment (e.g., when hungry, the baby may lead mother into the kitchen and point to the refrigerator). You want to find out whether imitative behavior occurred as the baby became more organized, and whether he showed signs of internalizing (for example, limits), perhaps by beginning to respond to "No." You want to know if the child went through this developmental stage and how the parents reacted to it.

Next, you want to find out when the child began displaying the capacity to represent things mentally. One sign of this capacity is the beginning of language at 18 to 24 months. Mahler talks about this as the rapprochement phase of development, and Piaget as the development of object permanence —the child can find an object that is well hidden. In this phase the child's developing mental representational capacity is evidenced by language, a greater capacity for recall, and a greater capacity to hold onto experiences over time (e.g., emotional memory). More complicated patterns of organized behavior should emerge: in other words, the child should be able to form a multisensory image.

Mahler (1975) explains that a regression takes place along with the formation of this capacity for mental pictures. Interestingly enough, in his own language Piaget (1969) also refers to a regression, calling it a vertical decollage. That is, the child who has been acting like king or queen of the universe, feeling both independent and protected under the omnipotent umbrella, now becomes more clinging and dependent. Mahler suggests that this is partly because the toddler, being able to differentiate better, can now see more realistically his own size in relationship to the universe—that is, how small, weak, and helpless he is. Moreover, the capacity to represent things verbally and in mental symbols makes the child cease to feel a part of the parents' omnipotent umbrella.

Mahler describes the "ideal mother" for the rapprochement phase as one who can walk that ephemeral line between encouraging independence and yet being available to give the needed support and nurturance. She believes that children do reasonably well in this phase when parents respond intuitively and empathically to their increased dependency and need for support. Parents who see this dependency as a negative sign or a weakness in the child, however, sow the seeds of later character problems and neuroses, according to Mahler. Consequently, it is particularly important for you to know about the rapprochement phase in terms of the degree of the child's regression and the mother's reaction to it. How mother and father dealt with the child, how the child dealt with the new awareness, and in what ways the child dealt with stress during that rapprochement phase, all provide important indications of how the child's basic defense structure was going to develop.

The emergence of this new symbolic capacity essentially transforms the child. Whereas previously the child was a "behaving being," with only vaguely organized internal experiences, now the child is a thinking being. At this new level of organization, the child goes through a separation-individuation process once again, moving farther away, showing exploratory behavior, and coming back again. In libidinal terms, this is the anal phase of development, and actually, the title corresponds nicely to some of the tasks that are going on at the level of object relations. Many children are started on toilet training around this time and the organization of drives is shifting from oral to anal. There should be features of stubbornness and negativism, which arise not only from the stresses of the developmental tasks but also from the changes in basic drive organization.

During the second and third years, the child continues to elaborate and refine the mental representations of the self and the world. One should ask if the child developed representational capacity (i.e., thematic trends at a symbolic level—using words, play objects such as dolls, etc.) in all of life's emotional domains: love, dependency, pleasure, assertion, protest, anger, negativism, etc. If not, note which thematic trends were absent (e.g., no intimacy or no curiosity) and you will see the emergence of character limitations (rigidities).

It is also necessary for the child to differentiate the mental representations of the self from representations of the external world and the important loved objects, namely, the parents. This differentiation forms the basis of reality testing and other basic ego functions. It is a long process starting around 20 to 24 months and continuing till age 4 or 5. But by age 3½ to 4, reality testing certainly should be reasonably well established. For instance, at this age children should be involved in primary-process fantasy but, when you insist, should be able to test reality reasonably well. When you see a 3-year-old who is not moving in this direction, who is unable to differentiate self from nonself at an internal symbolic or representational level, you know he is having problems.

Referring to children aged 3½ to 4, Mahler describes the attainment of what she calls libidinal object constancy, that is, the capacity of the child to maintain a *constant* delineated representation of self and a *constant* delineated representation of significant loved ones in terms of a mental form or psychological structure. The child who has achieved the stage of libidinal object constancy has a sense of security that he never had before. The child does not need the continuous presence of the parent to feel secure because he can now maintain an inner representation of the parent. This capacity forms the basis not only of this important sense of security but also of the internalization of control in regulating body functions, impulses, etc. Without attaining a consolidated sense of libidinal object constancy (which is never attained 100 percent—it is always a relative thing) to an age-appropriate degree, it is very hard for a child to move on to the next stages of development, because the capacity for libidinal object constancy is a foundation for the basic ego functions that evolve between ages 3 and 5, when secondary-process thinking becomes more organized. Your questions to the parents should focus on how the child dealt with separations, what happened when she was angry, and what happened when she started going to nursery school. When 3½- and 4-year-olds show a reaction of extreme panic, separation anxieties, or fears of the parents dying or never returning, it means that their capacity for libidinal object constancy is vulnerable.

Up to this point the child has been mainly involved in what can be called dyadic relationship patterns, that is, he sees the environment predominantly as a two-person system composed of himself and a significant other. The significant other is interchangeable, even though the child can distinguish between mother, father, playmates, and others. The key other may switch, but if the key other leaves or is destroyed, then the child has no one else, which is why the child in the dyadic phase experiences feelings like anger, jealousy, and envy as so frightening. With the attainment of object constancy, the youngster becomes able to move on—assuming there has been appropriate maturation of the central nervous system—to more complicated triangular relationship patterns, which are characteristic of the phallic-Oedipal phase of development.

What distinguishes the triangular relationship of the Oedipal phase is not that the child relates to more people, but that his relations have a different style and sophistication. Adding another counter to a game formerly played with two counters increases the number of available options by much more than 50 percent. It is important to note, however, that the presence of the familiar rivalries, intrigues, and secret agendas of a three-person system is not sufficient evidence of movement into the Oedipal phase of development. A child may talk about or show phallic concerns in play that are derivatives of the drives in the context of basically dyadic patterns. In fact, many adult schizophrenic and borderline patients create lives heavily laden with Oedipal fantasies in the context of dyadic relationships. Their wish to beat out father and to win mother is either in the context of receiving basic dependency support or in the context of a sadomasochistic dyadic struggle. These Oedipal-like behaviors are usually defenses against earlier, more primitive symbiotic issues of survival and maintaining a sense of being loved.

One way to know whether a child has moved on to three-person relationship patterns is to determine whether he has sufficiently resolved his two-person relationship systems. Look at basic ego functions, such as reality orientation; impulse regulation; affect organization; mood stabilization; the capacity to stay organized under stress; and the capacity for an age-appropriate range of affects, including the ability to deal with loss, separation, and disappointment. A very subtle sign of having progressed to the triangular stage of development is the capacity to integrate life's polarities: ego splitting is not used by the child who in one play session shows assertiveness, aggressive and passive modes, and hostile and pleasurable attitudes all as parts of one self. And then, of course, you look for evidence of genuine triangular relationships. Aspects of genuine triangular relationships are affects of love, curiosity, lust, jealousy, and an emerging capacity for real empathy.

Next you want to know to what degree the child has mastered the tasks of this (Oedipal) developmental stage and resolved his triangular relationships. You look to see if his world of intrigues, rivalries, and competitions became displaced into other spheres—at school, for example—or if, on the contrary, there was some resolution which freed him for the variety of endeavors typical of the latency period. The ideal resolution is the establishment of the superego, a psychological system that permits regulation of impulses as well as maintenance of self-esteem. You want to know to what degree the child's superego is internalized and consolidated; that is, to what degree he can regulate himself and reward himself for things well done, to what degree he has developed a sense of moral judgment as well as a sense of empathy.

If there is Oedipal resolution, internalization of some parental attributes, and a capacity for self-esteem, then you are seeing movement into latency-age activities, such as the ability to expand from family relationships to peer ones, to focus on school work, to follow the rules, and so on. The depth and stability of peer relationships, the capacity to delay and cope with frustration, the emerging sense of ideals, and the ability to learn without sacrificing a rich emotional life are all signs of the degree of progression into latency.

I have been describing some nodal points, or milestones, of early development. You need to have your own outline, or map, of development from birth to adolescence, which should contain all the major lines of development and all the nodal points that you think are important. Use this internal outline to guide your history-taking from the parents and to ask specific questions about what happened in major areas of development. Obviously, children's reactions to the birth of siblings, toilet training, weaning, and other routine experiences should all be explored.

What you want to have at the end of your history-taking is information on all the categories that we used for the initial diagnostic interview—the categories of physical and neurological integrity, mood, affects, relationships, communication patterns, thematic organization, etc. If you can develop a picture of how these categories of functioning evolved over time and at what point a child stopped operating in a developmentally appropriate way in any of these categories, it will help you greatly in your diagnosis. A child who stopped developing in a number of major categories (e.g., relationships, affects, mood, thematic style) at age 3½ is quite different from a child who progressed to age 7 and then lost some of his capacities to grow. A child whose progress stopped only in terms of the range of certain affects is very different from a child who stopped progressing in a number of basic categories, e.g., relationships, thematic organization, and aspects of physical-neurological functioning.

I hope this discussion has made clear how the historical perspective complements your direct observations of the child's developmental level in each area of functioning. For a more detailed discussion and framework of early development which covers both emotional and cognitive growth, you may want to consult *Intelligence and Adaptation* and *Psychopathology and Adaptation in Infancy and Early Childhood* (Greenspan, 1979; in press). A brief outline of the major points covered in the developmental history is presented below.

### Summary Outline of Areas to be Covered in Developmental History

1. Overall patterns in relation to developmental experiences:
   a. Early homeostatic regulatory patterns (e.g., apathetic, hyperirritable, engaged and interested in the world, withdrawn), establishment of rhythms and cycles
   b. Early experiences of comfort, care, and protection
   c. Early feeding and weaning (from breast or bottle)
   d. Early attachment or lack of fit, style, intensity
   e. Early differentiating experiences
   f. Early experiences for organized, assertive, original behavioral patterns (e.g., In second year could the patient (P) engage in complex games and behavioral interactions? Could P take caretaker by the

hand and show him or her what P wanted, rather than simply crying? Were emotions complex and rich, incorporating positive and negative feelings, or did one polarity dominate?)

g. By the second year of life and beginning of third year of life, did initiative and identification patterns lead to internal representational capacities, as evidenced by indications of fantasy life, in addition to cognitive capacities for language, personal pronouns, etc.?

h. During third and fourth year, did reality orientation and greater capacity for self-care begin to replace earlier magical thinking and/or regressive tendencies, such as extreme negativism or lack of impulse control?

i. During fourth through sixth years, did relationship patterns expand, did curiosity and interest expand (e.g., in the human body, sexual differences in the parents, relationships); did emotions become richer and more complex, showing greater capacity for empathy?

j. Did participant enter latency, psychologically speaking, from the perspective of interests and wishes, capacities for self-control and regulation, moral development, school and learning performance, etc.?

k. Similarly, after latency, assess stages of puberty, early adolescence, etc., to present stage of development

l. In addition, when not already presented, obtain data on the following experiences:
   (1) birth of siblings
   (2) toilet training
   (3) initial experiences of separation (e.g., going to school, being placed for temporary/foster care)
   (4) significant separations or losses (death, illness, divorce)

2. Special additional focus (where not already covered) should be directed to the following areas:
   a. History of establishing relationships in the early years of life: whether P was withdrawn and very passive versus friendly and lovable; whether P formed intense attachments with parents or parent surrogates versus being "promiscuous" in terms of attachment
   b. Patterns of relationships with siblings, peers, parents as P was growing up, including exploration of patterns appropriate for each developmental phase (e.g., Did P get involved with other peers and go from

parallel to interactive play? Did relationship patterns shift from dyadic to triangular and posttriangular patterns?

3. Any major illnesses, including emotional illnesses, in P's life

4. Development of affects and impulse control
   a. Any indications of aggressive or sadistic behavior, or poor impulse control
   b. Any indications of ability to experience sadness and mourning in the first 4 to 5 years of life or later
   c. Comfort with assertiveness, passivity, and feelings of loss

5. Feelings about own body, bodily processes; feelings and thoughts about sex; sexual experiences, etc.

### Talking to Parents about Your Recommendation

Let us assume that you have assessed the multiple lines of the child's development in terms of age-appropriate accomplishments, that you have made a diagnosis, and that you have reached a conclusion about the type of treatment needed. It is now time to make your recommendations to the parents. You should know that many (some suggest at least 50 percent) parents do not follow the recommendations, often because of the family dynamics. It is therefore extremely important that you work with these dynamics as part of the evaluation process.

At this point, you already have an impression of the parents, either from your sessions together or from another clinician who has worked with the parents. It is beneficial to reassess the parents. Let them start off the session. See what their concerns are, where their associations lead, what kind of questions they have. Do not start it off yourself by telling them what you have found. A lot has happened between the first time you saw them and now. Let them bring you up to date: Have they seen any changes in the child? Have their concerns remained the same, or changed? Get them to talk so you can see where they are now. If they seem to have trouble starting the discussion, say something general, such as, "I expect you have some questions," or "Are there things you have been thinking about?"

It is particularly important to determine whether there is any parental resistance to hearing what you have to say or to the idea of beginning treatment, if that is your recommendation. If there is some resistance, focus on it. Do not skip over it. When you skip over it, you are just satisfying yourself: you are talking so that you can finish a process. If there is resistance, simply making recommendations is not going to break it down. The way to deal with parental resistance is to let the parents ask whatever questions they may have first. If they begin by prodding you, saying, for instance, "Look, doctor, we are just interested in what you found. We have talked enough in this process. Now it is your turn to talk," ask them to specify in more detail the particular areas that concern them, explaining that you want to make sure that you answer their questions. Tell them that you can and will describe the child, but in doing so you want to make sure you do not miss anything that is important to them. And again, as you hear them describing their concerns, you will pick up resistance, you will pick up denial, you will pick up distortions. Then you can talk to them about these issues.

For instance, they may have originally presented the child to you as depressed and sad, and now they say that he is happy and his only problem is that he is not reading well in school—thus denying their initial concerns about the child's emotionality. This is an opportunity to say, "I gather you've changed your mind. Your impression of him has changed from the first time we talked." And then they may say, "He is much better." You can respond, "Tell me about that. I am eager to know." If done properly, your comments will not be experienced as threatening. You are not saying, "Look, you are covering up. Your child is still sad and unhappy. How can you think he only has a reading problem?" You are not challenging the parents; you are simply a collaborator. You want to know how this child changed in their eyes. Maybe he really has changed. Maybe he was in a situational crisis and has come out of it; on the other hand, maybe the parents are employing denial and distortion. You have to help them integrate their earlier perceptions with their current one. If you do not help them, you are not going to have their support.

At this point you are constructing a bridge between the first session and the current session. Essentially what is needed is a restatement of what they see as the issues, which will provide an opportunity for you to work on resistance, distortion, denial, and so on. Encourage the parents to be as specific as possible about the child's original behavior, strengths and weaknesses, the child's feelings and their own. Basically, you want to help them with their observing ego because it is the parents who provide the observing ego for the child, particularly for the preadolescent. Whereas an adult patient brings his or her own observing ego to the therapeutic process, here the parents are the ones who will keep the treatment going if the child wants to quit. You want to get them to form an alliance with you on as factual and detailed a basis as possible.

After helping them overcome any resistance, your next goal is to enhance their understanding by giving them additional data. You can say, "Let me share some things that I have observed"—*observed,* not *concluded*—without even using the word "problem." You do not have to betray a confidence; you do not tell a particular content that the child disclosed. You talk about the child in all the categories that we outlined: the way he organizes communications; his physical and neurological behavior; the kinds of affects the child shows. This approach helps the parents look at the child in a more differentiated way. They begin thinking of the child in terms of his emotions, moods, and activity level, as well as the things he talks about. You want to elaborate as rich and detailed a picture as possible, and to communicate in a way that they can understand and that corresponds with the picture they are trying to describe. You are helping the parents to be better observers of their child—a very useful therapeutic aid.

Again, you have an opportunity to see where there is resistance. As the parents focus more on the child's reading problems in school, giving mere lip service to the fact that he is also depressed at home and has trouble asserting himself with peers, you can say, "You know, we are both mentioning these issues, but I have a feeling you are more concerned about the school problems than about the problems he has with friends on the block. I am concerned about relationships with the friends on the block. I wonder why we have these differences in emphasis." This approach focuses their attention on their denial and allows you to see how much resistance there is. It may be mild. The next series of associations may begin with the father saying, "I was just like that when I was a kid. I also couldn't compete with the other kids and I would stay close to home." Often that kind of disclosure will serve to make the father feel comfortable talking to you. That is an example of mild resistance. In another family there may be immense denial: they may insist that the problem is the child's reading. It is crucial that you deal with the resistance for as long as it takes. If you cannot help them overcome it in one session, then see the parents two, three, ten times if necessary. Sometimes you have to see them repeatedly if you want treatment to begin; otherwise, you know they will not take your recommendation.

Now if you are in a clinic that limits the number of times you can see the parents, you may not be able to have as many sessions as needed to reach agreement on what the issues are. If the family is likely to flee because they are now denying that there is a problem, you can say at the end of the time, "Look, we haven't reached any agreement, but we have learned an awful lot about the child. I think we ought to take more time to share it. I can't be the one to do it with you, but I will introduce you to the person who will. She will have a little more time and can go over the diagnostic material with you. I think we should take as much time as necessary to understand what Johnny's situation is, so you can reach a decision about whether Johnny needs help." In this way you can delay the parents' reaching a decision for as long as a year while they bring Johnny in regularly for his "extended diagnostic" sessions. Even if they refuse to bring Johnny, at least the parents are coming, and you can focus on the diagnostic feedback for as long as it takes for them to recognize their child's problem at a descriptive level.

In other words, treatment, if indicated, begins with agreement on step one, and parents and child should not skip step one for the clinician's sake (so the clinician can feel his job is done and then say, "The family is resistant"). As indicated, therapeutic work can begin as an extended diagnostic consultation, no matter how long it takes. There is no such thing as an untreatable family if the family is willing to come in for extended diagnostic consultations.

When you reach some agreement with the parents at a descriptive level you should then discuss the developmental level. Do not offer the parents dynamic formulations about problems of aggression, and so forth. These are not conducive to their collaborating with you to facilitate the child's development. Put the information into a developmental context, again using the categories that I suggested earlier. Show them where and why Johnny is at appropriate developmental levels or below in each category. Such an approach provides a nonthreatening way for parents to hear about their child's problems, and you can tell parents about fairly pathological things in that context. For example: "Your child relates to other people more like a two-year-old. The way he clings to you and is very negativistic is more like a two-year-old. There are certain kinds of experiences that may help him operate more like a six-year-old." They hear references to age-level activities in school constantly, so such references provide an easy way for them to understand that their child has difficulties. Such a statement is certainly

191

far less frightening than saying that their child is "disturbed": it communicates the same information, but more constructively.

Next, where possible, you may want to point out family patterns that are undermining the child's development and suggest alternative patterns that may facilitate his development, again using your clinical judgment about what is appropriate. Here you will most likely suggest areas for the parents to work on over a longer period of time in their collaboration in the child's treatment. Finally, at the successful conclusion of all this discussion, you can make your treatment recommendations. By this time such recommendations will be based on a common understanding and therefore may be readily accepted by the parents. After you make your treatment recommendation, listen to their associations for any further resistances, questions, or doubts. If you sense ambivalence, schedule another appointment.

Again, if you sense ambivalence but can no longer see the parents because the case has to be transferred, it is most important to recognize the ambivalence. Tell them that you sense they are still not fully in agreement with what you are saying, that you cannot meet with them again, but that another person will discuss the disagreement. Emphasize that it is best to resolve these issues before starting the therapy.

I cannot state too emphatically that step one in the treatment process is to gain collaboration at some level (even unconscious) on the problem issues and treatment goals. If parental distortion or denial makes such collaboration impossible, then working with the parents is the first and foremost goal. Parents who have grossly distorted views of their children are probably creating a maladaptive environment. An extended series of diagnostic consultations is the proper and excellent beginning in such a situation. Giving your feedback factually, with little regard for what the parents are able to hear and integrate, may take care of your need to complete the job, but in fact you are avoiding—just as the parents may be avoiding—the real task.

In summary, in this chapter we have discussed aspects of the interview with the parents. In addition to giving you an understanding of the "presenting problems" and past history, the clinical interview with the parents must be used to assess their functioning—both individually and as a family —and to deal with personal and family patterns that may undermine their "hearing" and following through on your recommendations.

# References

American Psychiatric Association. *Diagnostic and Statistical Manual of Mental Disorders,* 3rd ed. (DSM-III). Washington, D.C., 1980.

Brazelton, T. B. *Neonatal Behavioral Assessment.* National Spastic Society Monographs, Clinics in Developmental Medicine #50. London: William Heinemann & Sons, 1973. (Distributed in the United States by J. B. Lippincott Co., Philadelphia.)

Erikson, E. H. *Childhood and Society.* New York: Norton, 1950.

Freud, A. Normality and Pathology in Childhood: Assessments of Development. *The Writings of Anna Freud,* 6. New York: International Universities Press, 1965.

Greenspan, S. I. A Consideration of Some Learning Variables in the Context of Psychoanalytic Theory: Toward a Psychoanalytic Learning Perspective. [*Psychological Issues,* Monograph 33.] New York: International Universities Press, 1975.

Greenspan, S. I. Intelligence and Adaptation: An Integration of Psychoanalytic and Piagetian Developmental Psychology. [*Psychological Issues,* Monograph 47/48.] New York: International Universities Press, 1979.

Greenspan, S. I. Psychopathology and Adaptation in Infancy and Early Childhood: Principles of Clinical Diagnosis and Preventive Intervention. New York: International Universities Press, in press.

Mahler, M. S., Pine, F., and Bergman, A. *The Psychological Birth of the Human Infant, Symbiosis and Individuation.* New York: Basic Books, 1975.

Nagera, H. *Early Childhood Disturbances, The Infantile Neurosis and the Adult Disturbances.* New York: International Universities Press, 1966.

Piaget, J. *The Psychology of the Child.* New York: Basic Books, 1969.

# Index

# INDEX

196

# INDEX

# INDEX

# INDEX

# About the Authors

STANLEY I. GREENSPAN, M.D. is a child and adult psychoanalyst and psychiatrist. He is also Chief of the Mental Health Study Center, National Institute of Mental Health, and Associate Clinical Professor of Psychiatry and Child Health and Development at the George Washington University School of Medicine. Dr. Greenspan has authored or edited six books and monographs, and some forty articles. He is also the recipient of the Blanche F. Ittleson Award of the American Psychiatric Association for outstanding research contributions in the field of child psychiatry.

NANCY THORNDIKE GREENSPAN is a Health Economist with the Department of Health and Human Services. After completing her undergraduate education at Mount Holyoke College, she went on to do graduate work and research in health economics and has published a number of articles in this field.

| DATE | | | |
|---|---|---|---|
| | | | |
| | | | |
| | | | |
| | | | |
| | | | |
| | | | |
| | | | |
| | | | |
| | | | |
| | | | |
| | | | |
| | | | |